A World We Don't Want

Dystopia has become reality.
Be the Protagonist.

Peter Vasey

Paperback: 978-1-9193792-0-3

eBook: 978-1-9193792-1-0

Audiobook: 978-1-9193792-2-7

Dedication

For PJ, who got me into computers,

Bev, my wonderful wife, who encouraged me to turn it into a profession,

Richard, who suggested I was on to something,

and to my incredible son, Ben, for whom I hope I am wrong.

Foreword

Forewords are usually written by someone you've heard of to endorse what you're about to read (or considering reading), particularly if the author of the book is not well known.

As you've never heard of me, this Foreword will disappear from the draft once a proper celeb has been found, but as someone who has the privilege to know Pete, and the greater privilege to have read this book early, I thought I'd drop my placeholder in.

Having worked with and for Pete, I know him to be a man who cares. Cares for his customers, cares for his colleagues, cares for his family, and as you will read, cares for this planet and its inhabitants.

In well-reasoned and passionate terms, he shows how far we've disappeared down the road to dystopia, while also revealing his expert solution focus with practical advice to drag us back from the brink.

This is not an extended rant against technology – after all, his day job is helping organisations adopt AI – but it shows how we always need to be mindful in everything.

I hope this book will positively affect all who read it, and that together we'll improve our world for future generations.

– Rick Eveleigh, Buckinghamshire

Contents

Introduction

Orwell, Huxley, and Bradbury all saw failings in the way society was evolving. We read their books, watched the movies, and considered them to be great entertainment, but we are now at a crucial point where signs from their dystopian worlds are already visible in the real world, and we appear to be happily heading towards something darker.

This book is not about the world being irreparably broken, no, I have laid out my observations, question if it is already too late to change course and discuss what we can do to prevent further decline.

1984 is arguably one of the best known and familiar of all dystopian titles and I admit that I knew as much about it as the majority of people; Big Brother, oppression, Room 101, surveillance, fear, etc., but not what the real message of the book was about or how it played out. Orwell was clearly calling out concerns he held about the future and our direction of travel, and for a piece of work written in 1949, it is certainly visionary. Some of the things he wrote about felt too close to home and it made me think about today's world.

I realised that this was much more than a good novel based in a fictional dystopian land. As I pieced together the parts from the novel, today's world, and my thoughts, *1984* changed from being just a famous dystopian novel and good entertainment to a clear warning for society. I was not aware at this point that it would turn into anything more.

My cheerful reading stint continued with Huxley's *Brave New World*, a book that was recommended to me by a friend as a juxtaposition to Orwell's surveillance, oppression and fear-based dystopia. *Brave New World* is a bit of a hard read at the start and takes some persistence, but as it gains momentum it talks about the seeding of formative information and conditioning of human minds. It is based in a highly engineered class society with a populace that is subjected to the manipulation of happiness. *Brave New World* is about maintaining a superficial and shallow happiness through the removal of one's desire. The people are kept in their place in society and are conditioned to be content in what they were 'created' to do. Yes, the humans in *Brave New World* are created to maintain balance in the classes and uniformity. And once again I found myself feeling that parts of the book were a little uncomfortable.

The last novel I chose to read as part of this happy trilogy was Bradbury's *Fahrenheit 451*. I knew it was a well-known dystopian novel, but I had no prior knowledge of the pretence or preconceived ideas about the message.

1984 uses surveillance, misinformation, and fear. *Brave New World* uses engineered happiness and chemical pacification. *Fahrenheit 451* is more about the populace 'choosing ignorance'. This is a very different approach, it felt more 'real world', and by the end of it I had drawn further, similar, and stronger conclusions about the relationship of these three books to today's world. And I didn't like the pattern that was forming.

Whilst not one of these authors got it exactly right, as a collective they were certainly on to something. They were warning us about the perils for the society of the future based on what they could see emerging. I started comparing these prescient novels to what I see as a technical, business and change consultant, as a father, and as a member of society. I concluded that they'd all got parts of the vision right, but the picture being painted when all three were combined was both striking and terrifying. We face a global crisis with drastic and long-term effects, societally, economically, politically, and mentally.

Look around the world as it is today and you will see direct comparisons with each novel; I will explore these through this book to help build out the picture.

Technology is everywhere and screens are abundant; we carry them around with us, they are by our beds at night, we use them for both play and work, and for incredible amounts of time. And whilst they might not be used directly for recording and monitoring our every move or word as in *1984*, they are used to generate huge volumes of valuable data about us and what we do, where we go, and who we interact with. They show us constant streams of news, information, manipulated truths, and entertainment, in specially designed 'easy to consume' formats. Social media platforms and inherently biased algorithms go to reinforce and actively support our existing views rather than showing alternative viewpoints. Our attention spans have dropped dramatically and are dropping still further. We prefer to consume nuggets of information rather than explore and learn through study or experiment. We have access to a great breadth of information but not true knowledge, and the quality of the information we consume is lesser, inadequate, inaccurate, and is frequently manipulated into a 'mistruth', or lie as it used to be called.

This book features and acknowledges the works of Orwell, Huxley, and Bradbury, as they were onto something big, as I am sure many others were, but I want to lay out what we were told in those novels and align it to the patterns and behaviour we are seeing today. All these things, and more, are having an impact on society, employment, education, and are creating a change in our mindset that is detrimental to our future as a species.

Part 1 sets the scene, Part 2 talks about those three great dystopian novels: *1984*, *Brave New World*, and *Fahrenheit 451*. Ironically, and you will find out why that is the case later, I have summarised the key points for those who haven't read them. Part 3 looks at the array of problems that we, as a society, are facing today; things that have been introduced by or accelerated through our use of and reliance on technology. Part 4 discusses the real-world impacts of those challenges on society, business, education, and so on. Part 5 sees an upturn in tone, I look at what we, as the potential protagonists of our global society, can do to stop the slide from where we are now to a true, novel worthy, dystopian society and how we can explore positive ways to help us prevent this becoming an irreversible shift.

And finally, Part 6 summarises this book, shares my conclusions and what we should do next, and introduces the concept of the Dystopian Delta to help gauge our distance from a full dystopia.

Please take this book with the intent with which it has been written. It is not an academic research book, and it is not an outright business book. It is more of a follow-on warning for society, but with guidance on how we might mitigate the deepening of our own dystopia. With the help of these prescient novels, I discuss the challenges depicted in them, how they align to today's world, and ask serious questions about what we are doing.

It is already possible to see the early signs of the decline in society, signs that cannot remain unchecked and unaddressed. Our ability to learn, critically think, and challenge information is eroding away, and the impact on society is far from good. I hope you will start to see what I see: a future of intellectual decline and apathy. One I believe we have already entered, hence the title of this book.

I really hope I'm wrong, and if I am, thanks for taking the time to read this book; but if I'm right, then maybe as a global collective we can do something together to halt the decline.

I hope you find this book interesting and thought provoking.

Part 1 - The Definition of Dystopia

A broken society, born of the negative consequences of unchecked power and technological advancements; governed by a ruling elite who derive control over people through misinformation, surveillance, technological manipulation, and the suppression of thought.

Founded on compliance, ignorance and superficial contentment; where the general populace is easily appeased, distracted, and fooled; and where dehumanisation and hate lead to the demise of mental and physical well-being.

It is a world that is undesirable and filled with unemployment, poverty, suffering and injustice.

Chapter 1 – Dystopian Warnings

The dystopian future has been a staple of the literary and cinematic worlds for centuries. Quite what is so compelling about portraying a view of the future that is corrupted, broken, dysfunctional and often violent, I don't know, but here I am talking about it, researching it, and now I have written a book about it. So, there must be something to it.

Your typical dystopian novel or movie will contain a set of common features: a powerful organisation or corporation in control of society, a vivid picture of how control is established and maintained, a protagonist or two to fight against the system, an ending that does not result in the downfall of the oppressors, and of course, an element of hope. Let's face it, without a protagonist and a glimmer of hope the novels would be nothing more than a collection of depressing views of the future.

The novels focus on the way control is exerted and maintained, the mechanisms and methods employed, the harsh consequences of contravention, rebellion or disobedience, and the personal journeys of the protagonists and their route to enlightenment. Most dystopian movies follow similar patterns but tend to focus on a sensationalised version of what society might be or look like, often portraying a significant underground movement, vast poverty and unemployment, and the presence of a sub-class living in squalid conditions.

In any society that dares to call itself civilised this sub-class should not exist; there has always been a divide between the 'haves and have-nots', but it is accelerating and growing to a level that we have never seen. It is a very real problem; a rapidly developing sub-class of our own making, but this time the divide between the haves and have-nots is higher than ever before. Even those who have had a good education are starting to be directly impacted and this is set to deepen further in the coming years. I'll explain more as we go through the book, but whilst the idea of people living in sewers might seem far-fetched, the general concept of 'those without' is alive, growing, and very much present today, if not fully recognised and understood.

Modern society is increasingly, and very rapidly, being shaped by technological advancements, and we now find ourselves at a critical juncture. The warnings laid out by Orwell, Huxley, and Bradbury seem to be coming to fruition, if they haven't already set down permanent roots. All three novels contain themes that can be applied to society today, with additional relevance and pace since the emergence of Generative AI (Gen AI), social media, and our seeming dependence on screens.

We can see the engineered pleasure and conditioning, the willing surrender of knowledge and cognitive freedom, the frequent manipulation of truth, pervasive surveillance, the loss of critical thought, and the rise of societal apathy. I start with the following chapters that provide summaries of each of the three novels. Again, the level of irony in that statement will become very clear.

Part 2 – The Great Dystopian Novels

Chapter 2 – 1984

Oceania, the fictional setting created by George Orwell, is governed by 'The Party', an autocratic and totalitarian regime that has absolute power and control over its citizens. The Party's ideology is based on a well-established and absolute control over every aspect of a citizen's life, including thought. Society is divided rigidly into three very distinct classes, each with their place and role in society. They use 'telescreens' that are located everywhere, in every room, and provide an all-encompassing surveillance that sees and hears everything you do or say. It is not impossible to escape the watchful presence of a telescreen for a short period of time, but even if you succeed, your movements and social interactions will have been tracked and observed. Constant surveillance is core to the Party's control of the citizens, but their control extends far further and includes the manipulation of the truth, altering history to suit The Party's narrative, and preventing access to anything that might jeopardise their power.

In addition, telescreens continually disseminate Party approved content and propaganda; they are depicted as showing that same approved content on all screens simultaneously, in a form of brainwashing. The content conditions minds and maintains the citizens' fear of The Party, thereby ensuring acceptable behaviour. It is about communicating, not the truth, but what The Party want the citizens to know.

The head figure of The Party is 'Big Brother'. Hence the famous phrase 'Big Brother is watching you'. Although it is never made clear in the novel if Big Brother is a person or not, it is a visible role, a humanisation or fabricated face of The Party, something that is viewed as benevolent, all seeing, all powerful, and all knowing, but certainly not kind. A persistent face of power that is used to maintain the consistency required to keep the citizens in their place.

At the top of the societal tree is the Inner Party, the ruling elite who hold the highest positions of power and privilege. Think of them as your government and politicians. They, of course, enjoy a life of luxury, with unfettered privilege, access to information that is not available to others, fine foods, servants, and most importantly, they are able to turn off their telescreens when they desire privacy.

It is a clear demonstration of the highest levels of hypocrisy by the Inner Party and reflects the ruling elite's indifference to the supposed egalitarianism that they portray externally. The Inner Party are, without doubt, the driving force behind the authoritarian rule.

Subject to them are the Outer Party members, who are essentially the middle classes. They carry out the Party's will and ensure that the lower classes remain obedient, but unlike the Inner Party members, they themselves are subject to constant surveillance through the telescreens. They face chronic shortages of essentials and basic goods, and their living conditions are portrayed by Orwell as simple and pretty poor. Keeping the Outer Party members in this environment allows the Party to foster a sense of fear and mistrust, compelling them to unwaveringly follow the ideology set out by the Inner Party, and to actively participate in the further oppression of the class below them, the Proles.

The Proles, or Proletariat, make up the vast majority of the citizenry. They are the uneducated masses, the working classes, and are almost entirely disregarded by the Party, who treat them like animals and as no significant threat, primarily due to their lack of education. Oddly, due to that lack of education and perceived lack of threat, the Proles are granted more freedom from surveillance than Party members. They are perceived as being incapable of organising any resistance. Their daily life is portrayed as pretty miserable, manual labour for poor wages, struggling to make ends meet, and only finding small moments of joy in the simplest of pleasures like movies, football, beer, and gambling; all of which are Party approved activities of course. They have virtually no access to resources or amenities, and they lack any real political awareness. They are more concerned about the small things in life than larger injustices, and that makes them easy to distract.

The Party relies on the notion that revolution requires organised thought and collective identity. The Proles, with their limited education and lack of access to information and learning, along with their poor living conditions, are not considered capable of this kind of thought. By granting them petty freedoms and superficial and shallow entertainment the Party can appease them just enough to prevent dissent.

The Party reserves its most brutal and comprehensive controls for those considered to be intellectually capable, in other words, the Outer Party members who could pose a threat if allowed independent thought or strong relationships, and it employs a sophisticated approach to the control and appeasement of its citizens. Displays of disobedience are met with fierce consequence, but their desire is the complete eradication of independent thought and emotional autonomy. The combination of total surveillance and fear are the foundations of control; citizens live under constant observation with their every movement, sound, and even facial expressions being monitored. It is a truly dark way to create constant fear, and something that leads to a form of self-censorship, for fear of the consequences.

This is taken further by the existence of the 'thought police', depicted as an omnipresent and unseen force; nasty and insidious, they indiscriminately torture, imprison, and 'vaporise' (or shall we say 'disappear') anyone whose thoughts or actions even suggest they might commit a crime in the future. With no formal laws they can deliver compliance through terror.

Propaganda is another of the core mechanisms used to control reality and shape the 'perception of truth'. The Ministry of Truth, where the main protagonist works, is dedicated to distorting history and facts. This distortion ensures that the Party's narrative is the only accepted reality, and it creates an unquestioning populace that is conditioned to and subject to their manufactured reality. This is very clever as it means that the Party can indiscriminately use terror on anyone because it always aligns to the manufactured truth. If you have taken a liking to squeaky toys, and the Party doesn't like it, the truth will be altered so that squeaky toys are a threat and, bingo, you are now subject to the will of the thought police.

Interestingly, the novel refers to the fact that the Party also engineered its own language, constantly altering and simplifying words to limit an individual's thought and speech. This makes it near impossible to form the concept of rebellion or shape ideas against the Party's, because it is literally impossible to articulate; the words no longer exist. The removal of words like 'freedom' or 'individuality' renders any potential rebel unable to describe what they are thinking. If it doesn't exist, it can't be talked about and therefore can't happen.

The weapons available to the Party are extensive and diverse; it is very well thought through, albeit vicious. Psychological manipulation, where individuals are compelled to hold two contradictory ideas and believe both to be true, is used repeatedly throughout the novel. It systematically erodes logical reasoning and goes towards fostering a deeper loyalty by making it impossible for citizens to discern truth from falsehood.

Personal relationships and sex are also controlled in Oceania and sexual relationships are policed. It is thought that hysteria, caused by sexual frustration, could be harnessed into 'war fever and leader-worship'. The formation of strong personal and emotional bonds could divert loyalty away from the Party to another human being, and love, as we know, can be a powerful motivation.

The final method I want to call out is what is seen as the ultimate enforcement mechanism: torture, both physical and mental. This is the primary punishment for rebellion. It is used not just to gain confessions but to fully achieve the Party's totalitarian ideology. Individuals are systematically broken, and their love or feelings for anyone else are destroyed and replaced with an enforced love for Big Brother. This is something that can certainly be seen in the authoritarian regimes and dictatorships of today's world.

The all-encompassing approach demonstrated by the Party is a direct and calculated target on human nature's vulnerabilities. Physical torture, fear, psychological manipulation, control of relationships and control of language and truth their approach targets every part of the human existence. It delivers behavioural control and ensures conformity, or at least the perception of conformity, and it suppresses acts of rebellion. It limits thought by the removal of vocabulary, destroys logical reasoning and objective reality, and along with the manipulation of history and truth, ensures the Party is always right, and therefore infallible.

It is a comprehensive system that aims to reshape human nature itself, while demonstrating a terrifying depth of totalitarian ambition.

Chapter 3 – Brave New World

The 'World State' is the equivalent of the Party in Orwell's *1984*. *Brave New World* presents a vision of a future totalitarian society where individual liberty is subtly usurped by an all-powerful state. The World State's motto is 'Community, Identity, Stability', and control is primarily achieved by convincing citizens to embrace their servitude through what is referred to as engineered 'happiness'.

Society is organised into a rigid caste system, comprising of five main castes: Alphas, Betas, Gammas, Deltas, and Epsilons. Each caste is assigned different tasks or jobs, which they have been conditioned to perform in order to uphold the stability of this supposedly perfect society. The Alphas and Betas make up the intellectual ranks and leadership and are genetically engineered to be physically and intellectually superior so they can undertake the more complex tasks.

The Gammas, Deltas, and Epsilons are intellectually and physically inferior; they are 'produced' in batches and conditioned for manual labour and menial tasks.

Life, for all castes, is controlled and engineered for constant gratification and conformity. Conditioning starts before birth and is both physical and psychological. It develops a human who is content with their designated place in society and their predetermined role. The conditioning is a continuous process, is broad in scope, and covers many aspects of life including the promotion of instant gratification, the benefits of casual sexual promiscuity where 'everyone belongs to everyone else' and embeds the opinion that constant economic consumption is good.

Unlike the other two novels, *Brave New World* introduces the widespread use of a government-issued drug called Soma. Soma ensures that any unpleasant experiences are immediately nullified. Immersive, sensory films provide intense but shallow entertainment, and any sign of traditional art, history, and religion have been eradicated and suppressed to prevent critical thought or dissatisfaction.

A key point in *Brave New World* is the existence of 'the Savage Reservation', an area that has been deliberately preserved and where the technologies and conditioning of the World State have not been introduced. Traditional human experiences like natural birth, gods, physical pain, and emotional suffering all still exist, making it an almost zoo-like experience that is only available to a select few. It is a symbol of natural humanity and cultural preservation and is used to highlight the trade-offs between comfort and authentic human experience. It is interesting that Huxley decided to retain this unspoiled human element within his dystopian world. It comes into play quite late in the book and serves a key purpose but raises the question whether the reserve was there to serve the purpose that it does, or whether it was really to show the arrogance and complacency of the World State, or both. Not that it makes much difference to where this book is going.

Engineered happiness and stability breeds dehumanisation; and the absence of suffering, genuine choice, and intense emotions lead to a shallow form of existence. In eliminating all suffering, strong emotions, deep desires, and meaningful relationships, the World State removes the very elements that contribute to depth, growth, and meaning in human life. Happiness, if you can call it that, is superficial, and in most cases chemically induced. Individuality is lost, critical thinking is suppressed, and all genuine human experience is eradicated.

This creates a subtle, insidious form of dystopian world, where people are essentially content in their 'slavery'. Huxley's warning was that society can be controlled more effectively through contentment and gratification than it can through pain and fear.

As mentioned, the psychological conditioning begins before birth where embryos, infant and young citizens fall subject to comprehensive neurological programming. Hypnopaedia (sleep-teaching) is used to good effect to shape desires, behaviours, social roles, and individuals' desires; ensuring that by the time they are old enough, they are content with their predetermined place in society and are unquestioning. By doing this the World State eliminates natural variation.

The birth process creates batches of identical twins, shaped for their specific tasks which results in a ready supply of compliant workers for every caste and raises ethical questions about the manipulation of human nature.

Brave New World is the only of the three novels to introduce the concept of pharmacological appeasement. The drug Soma is key to maintaining universal 'happiness'. It is government-issued, and provides an instant euphoria, eliminating all negative emotions and thereby preventing any discontent or rebellious thoughts. It provides a complete chemical escape. The hypnopaedia used so effectively in the early stages introduces phrases like 'a gramme is better than a damn' and it encapsulates the drug's role creating this chemically induced happiness in preference to any genuine experience or emotion. At points during the novel Soma comes to the proverbial 'rescue' to calm someone down or even induce a contented, albeit artificial, sleep.

The suppression of history, art, and culture is important in the prevention of critical thought and fostering contentment with the present. History is dismissed as 'bunk', and classic literature, philosophy, and religion are all banned, having been replaced by simplistic entertainment referred to as 'the feelies'. Erasing history prevents anyone comparing the society to past societies. You can't refer to the 'good old days' as they fundamentally never existed, which ensures that the present goes unexamined and uncontested.

The final element to consider is the use of instant gratification and the promotion of consumerisation to distract and control the populace. Citizens are conditioned to seek immediate pleasure and reward by participating in constant economic consumption. Shopping your way to happiness delivers a short lived and superficial contentment which continuously fuels the World State's economy through constant production and consumption.

Huxley's vision of control depicts a potentially more stable form of totalitarianism than Orwell's. Bleakly, this approach creates a population that 'loves its slavery' and is therefore less prone to rebellion. Huxley foresaw that true societal control could be achieved by making people so content with their superficial existence that they would lose their desire for genuine freedom, but he also warned of the potential consequences of unchecked scientific advancement and societal engineering.

Chapter 4 – Fahrenheit 451

The society depicted in *Fahrenheit 451* is markedly different from the other two novels and is characterised by ignorance, strict conformity, and society's mass addiction to mass media. Society is described as an empty shell of humanity, having chosen, and 'chosen' is the critical point, to disregard books and the knowledge contained within them. Books are obsolete thanks to the desire for short-form and summarised content.

As with *1984* and *Brave New World*, there is of course still a core principle of censorship and control, but this is achieved in *Fahrenheit 451* through the outlawing and destroying of books. The government and media exert an almost total control over information, and knowledge is managed to prevent independent thought. The overarching theme of the novel is the struggle between the desire for knowledge and individuality as experienced through the journey of the protagonist, versus the societal expectation of ignorance and conformity.

The populace is, again, largely working class and accepts society and the rules, it has been conditioned to resist knowledge, and there is a clear division between intellectuals and the ordinary people.

Now, for me, this is where things got very interesting. Life is dominated by mass media addiction and a lack of critical thought. People are constantly connected to mass media through devices worn in their ears and immersive rooms with wall-sized screens, providing continuous stimulation which distracts from deep thought, the processing of ideas, and noticing what's really going on; it stimulates the senses with programmes that lack any depth.

Society is addicted to immediate gratification and has developed a complete loss of interest in books and critical thinking. Reading, which requires time and cognitive effort, thought and consideration, holds no appeal.

Whilst the novel doesn't specifically call out a supreme or controlling body like the Party or World State, it does reference the clear exploitation, by the government, of the public's desire for easy gratification. This is capitalised on by the government who disseminate only mindless escapism via government approved media. The threat of the average citizen questioning authority is non-existent.

The story follows the main protagonist, Guy, who is a Fireman. Firemen in the context of this novel are enforcers of the system and are tasked with burning forbidden books rather than extinguishing fires. Guy encounters his neighbour who asks him simple, yet probing questions about happiness, nature, and the meaning of life. It is this encounter that opens Guy's eyes to the superficiality of society and drives him to seek greater meaning, which he believes is to be found in the books he is employed to burn. He defies the law, secretly collects and reads the books, and, as his awareness grows, he becomes increasingly discontent with the status quo. It is the pursuit of knowledge and his attempt to shed the ignorance that is so embraced by society that causes his life to turn upside down and spiral out of control.

Bradbury built his dystopia on wilful ignorance and resistance to change, and by doing so he paints a portrait of a society that prefers superficial contentment over intellectual engagement.

Control and appeasement are achieved through a combination of overt censorship of books and information, and the insidious and pervasive use of technology. Collectively they foster widespread ignorance and conformity.

The government exerts control through the systematic prohibition and burning of books. Without access to books, information, data, and the knowledge they can unlock, society loses the ability to think critically and independently. It creates a population that is easily manipulated and controlled. They are constantly bombarded with 'approved' information from the government and shallow, mass media without any means to verify or question it.

The novel highlights that this censorship, to a significant extent, is chosen by the people themselves, who opt for simplicity and a life without thought or the need to make decisions. By choosing to forgo knowledge and individuality they surrender their power to control their own future and become susceptible to manipulation.

Technology plays a crucial role in *Fahrenheit 451* by distracting the populace with shallow inane content; the rapid acceleration of technological capabilities, particularly in mass media, led to a society that was captivated by quick and easy consumption of entertainment and information. This addiction to immediate gratification triumphed over activities like reading, which required time and thought. It lost its appeal and as a result society lost its capacity for critical thinking, processing ideas, and developing unique identities.

The dangers of unguarded technological progress and media saturation run as a significant theme through the novel, suggesting that technology effectively destroyed the humanity of humans by eroding their capacity for intellectual engagement. In addition to this the novel also calls out that the dangers of technological progress are not merely about machines, but about how humans choose to interact with them. This is an interesting point which has led to a state where mass media facilitates censorship by making people too distracted or apathetic to seek knowledge or the truth.

Part 3 – The Signs of Dystopia

Chapter 5 – General Observations

Of course, the world has changed considerably since these novels were written. When *1984* was published in 1949, there was no real concept of the volume of screens and the advanced level of technologies that we have today. At the time of writing, *1984* would have been seen more as fiction than a prescient view of today.

By the 1990s and with the advent of the internet, computing began to reshape daily life. Bill Gates' vision of the future of a computer in every house and on every desk was starting to come true. By today's standards these technologies were still in their infancy, but they were starting to take hold, and, yes, connections were slow, computers lacked the processing power we now take for granted, but compared to where we had been this was quite something, and the rate of change that was emerging was of a scale we had not experienced before.

Fast forward to the 2000s, only ten years on, and the landscape was undergoing a dramatic transformation. 2007/8 saw the emergence of a new era; usable and reliable mobile data, high-speed broadband, and the introduction of smartphones revealed that a true turning point had been reached. Screens started appearing everywhere, on all sorts of devices. They were no longer just televisions at home, but they were in the workplace, shops, on advertising boards, and most importantly, in our pockets.

This introduced a whole new way of living. We could communicate almost instantaneously through text, voice and video, connect to almost anywhere in the world and across countless different platforms. We started to consume information and entertainment anytime, anywhere, and on any device. We no longer needed to retain knowledge or recall facts. And here is where we started to rewire our brains; technology brought with it great benefits and convenience, but it also led to major changes in our behaviours and society. Arguably, not for the better.

We communicate more now than ever before, however the emergence of shallow, short-form communication tools like SMS, and the informality of chat tools, have led to 'short-form' conversations. The quality of these communications has diminished our skills. For the younger generations this is their default way of communicating, but I believe it is a poor form of communication that is not fit for commercial, business, or general societal clarity. In conjunction with this change in how we communicate the art of casual debate is also being lost. Disputes over trivia and historical facts were once the cornerstone of lively interaction in pubs, workplaces, and social gatherings, but are now swiftly terminated by means of a quick internet search. These silly debates and discussions provided us with important life skills about debate and negotiation, and their decline has contributed to the erosion of our ability to communicate clearly.

The ease with which information and entertainment can be consumed has led to an addiction to technology and, more worryingly, certain applications. I am sure that many will argue to the contrary or outright deny it, but this addiction is visible everywhere. In cafes, pubs and streets, in parks and on trains, people everywhere stare at screens, play games, scroll through social media and consume huge volumes of cat videos, instead of interacting with the environment and those around them. Children can be seen competing for attention from adults who are glued to their devices, and we are controlled by notifications.

The screen obsession mirrors the conceptual use of screens in both *1984* and *Fahrenheit 451*, and the proliferation of screens in public and communal spaces aligns directly with *1984*. In situations where we desire the presence of screens and consume their content at our own free will, we align more closely to *Fahrenheit 451* and its portrayal of immersive rooms; big screens in rooms that provide 'quick and easy entertainment' that serves to distract.

Our love of apps and social media draw parallels with Soma, the government issued drug from *Brave New World* which creates artificial contentment and escapism. Entertainment, in the main, has become shallow and banal, and something that requires low cognitive effort. Our brains are being rewired for instant gratification and ease of consumption, rather than deep understanding, leading us to an increase in ignorance.

The rise of quick reference and bite-sized information prevents us from having to learn something new or perform our own research. We are increasingly consuming easy snippets of information without performing our own analysis, and that in itself raises serious concerns when technology can be manipulated so easily.

Manipulation and misinformation are rampant throughout the world, spread through social media, seemingly credible new outlets, fabricated news outlets, and many more avenues. Many platforms attempt to reinforce your existing beliefs in a 'if you liked that, you'll probably like this' approach, regardless of the accuracy of the information being surfaced. There is no desire to provide an alternative view because that is not what social media is about; it is about likes, clicks, the fight for your attention, and subscriptions. If you are left wing, there is a good chance you will be content to see and engage with more left-wing content, and that you will scroll past posts promoting right-wing activity.

Corporations of all sizes and shapes collect data: which sites you visit, how often, for how long, which ones you interact with, and so on. The level of data held on you is vast and often unknown or underestimated. Your mobile devices, smartphones, computers, applications, and browsers track everything you do, and even if you choose to use a private browser session, the search engine provider and the Internet Service Provider still know. There is a well-known saying that 'if you don't pay for the product, you are the product'.

All of this makes the information about you and your demographic data incredibly valuable to companies who will use this to hook you, and others like you, further into your addiction.

Because of this reinforcement approach to content, political and social views are diverging at an astonishing rate. If you hate, you will be subject to further pro-hate content and likewise any other topic. If you don't believe me, search social media and like a few pages on a topic you have no interest in. You will find that the topic will be thrown at you for the next few days. Social media and other platforms want to build ever stronger and tighter links.

Our thinking has been, and still is being, dramatically impacted. Search engines and Gen AI now mean that critical thinking is on the decline and is seen as becoming a less important skill. Instant answers and Gen AI are increasingly replacing traditional thought, deep engagement, and critical thinking. Information is being prioritised over wisdom, which is worrying as there is a fundamental difference between the two.

Gen AI is the first time a technology has really interfered and competed with human thought. We are starting to rely on AI tools and search engines for short summaries, which we know can be misleading. We are offloading our cognitive skills and are becoming unable to challenge the outputs, and this is creating a generation that is becoming ignorant and is mistaking *information* for *knowledge* or *wisdom*.

While books remain a truly valuable resource for those looking for self-improvement or development, the unchecked technological advancements and misuse of data raises serious concerns. Some organisations are collecting vast amounts of private data for marketing and other purposes, but this is furthering the social engineering and conditioning of the populace. Other organisations are very close to governments and are actively collecting information at a state level, something that has potentially drastic consequences for millions.

I will explore all these issues in detail over the coming chapters and provide examples to help highlight what is happening.

Chapter 6 – Communication

We're a complicated bunch, us humans. We have what is probably the most complex communication system of the entire animal kingdom, and this is because of two main factors; the first is that we don't know enough about how other species communicate, and the second is that no other species has created so many tools with which to communicate.

Whilst the development of communication tools is something that allows us to communicate wherever and whenever we like, the depth of experience is often lacking and use of them, poor.

We speak, use hand gestures and body language, we have intricate facial expressions and can communicate with our eyes, a timely sigh, or a hug. It is estimated that there are over 7,100 living, spoken languages in the world, and so when we meet others who don't speak the same language as us, we fill the gaps with gestures and smiles. We created written versions of our languages to help form a commonality in the use and meaning of words, and to allow us to communicate when we are not in the physical presence of another. Beyond these skills we have created great technologies that allow us to communicate over large distances, to individuals and large groups, via text, picture, voice, and video, and even to people out in space.

Communication is complex but, in general, there is a hierarchy of communication. Albert Mehrabian carried out a study in 1967 focussing on the inconsistency between verbal and non-verbal cues.

We use 100% of our natural communication stack when we speak face to face to someone, in a common tongue. The 100% involves all our facial expressions, gestures, body language, intonation, and of course the actual words. In genuine conversation all of this aligns to our chosen words, and when they don't align, we know something is wrong, out of place, or that someone is lying.

When we drop down the stack the richness and completeness of the communications lessen. Video provides a better experience than audio, and audio provides a better experience than text. But that is where we start to get into the murky realms of poor communication. We have created SMS, chat, memes, and emojis, all tools that encourage short-form or are limited in length by the platform.

In 2013 I wrote about how the next generations would communicate far more frequently but at a far lesser quality, and it feels like that is very much the case. There are now a dazzling array of social media messaging and chat tools available, and employees are faced with multiple different communication tools within the workplace. Some people prefer to use email as a more formal tool; others conduct business over informal or unapproved tools. Shadow IT appears because users don't find the business tools sufficient or quick enough to do their job. The Gen Z, Alpha, Beta, Jedi, or whatever it is, users are likely to communicate in a significantly different way to someone of 'more mature' years meaning there are notable gaps in the clarity of communication between different generations and/or education levels.

In short, communication is getting messy. Unfortunately, communication will be, without shadow of a doubt, the number one skill that is required to work in the modern world. Technology, for now, doesn't care how good your education was or wasn't, or how good your command of the language is, it will respond to what you ask it. If you don't ask it the right question, or give it the right command, or know how to ask it the question, you can expect the response to be out of sync with your expectations. If you get an answer you weren't expecting, go back and re-read your question or ask if you are likely to be the source of the problem.

Now consider this. We typically interact with Gen AI via text, one of the worst forms of communication we have available to us, and while there is a dramatic increase in verbal communication with Gen AI, to the Gen AI tool this is just a verbal input of text; no inflection, just the capture of words. So, whilst we can 'talk' to our AI assistants, the input is, in essence, still poor. For now, and for the foreseeable future, we are limited to one of the most basic forms of interaction with these tools. Does it really matter? Well, yes, I'm afraid it does matter quite a lot.

Here's a little test for you. Pick a topic that you know a bit about; you don't need to be an expert on the subject but know enough to be able to validate the output.

Write a prompt to be used with the Gen AI tool of your choice. Ask the question or give the prompt in a clear and structured manner. Microsoft recommend the GCSE structure: Goal, Context, Source and Expectation, so make sure your prompt has Goal, what you want to achieve; Context, so it understands what this is in relation to; provide it with reputable Sources to use; and set Expectations on what you want the output to be or look like. In addition to the GCSE structure, ask the Gen AI to assume the role of an expert in this field, run the prompt, look at the output and take notes.

Now rephrase that prompt into the way a child might ask, or a teenager, or someone who left school with no basic language qualification, someone speaking in their second or third language, or someone with learning difficulties. Drop out of the GCSE structure and expert role; compare the outputs and you will see that the answers vary greatly.

For example, your well-structured prompt might read as follows:

You are a world leading expert on climate change. You are being asked to contribute to a piece of research on the topic of climate change and its impact on wine production in the next 5 years. The goal of this report is to identify how the trend of rising temperatures and weather patterns will impact the growth, production and sugar content of grapes over the coming 5 years across the three main wine growing regions of the world.

The context is to produce a practical report that can be used to help wine makers determine what changes they need to make to the growth and nurture of vines, changes to the production, fermentation and processing of the grapes, and what the top recommendations are to mitigate any major downturn in production levels.

For the sources relating to wine, use only credible vine, vineyard, winery and vintner resources, that have an established history of more than 30 years in business. For the resources on climate change, use only international meteorological and established climate change organisations.

The Expectation is that the report will contain an Executive Summary, top 10 challenges, a summary per region, and the top 5 points to help mitigate a loss in production or quality.

In contrast, your lower quality version might be something like:

What is the relationship between climate change and wine production and what will the impact be in the next 5 years in the three main wine producing regions?

Feel free to copy that exact example for your own viewing. It should demonstrate that the command of the language is a clear determinator of how good your responses will be. Don't be afraid, or lazy. Challenge the findings it brings back to you. Treat it like a conversation.

When you are communicating with technology, you have no option to include intonation, facial expression, sarcasm, colourful language, or any of the other things that bring language to life, and yet this is the main tool we now use to communicate with Gen AI.

Our overall quality and ability to communicate properly is on the slide. Can we blame the pandemic? No, this was well underway before that. I recall witnessing a family member, sat on a video call to a friend, saying nothing, and messaging them in the background from another app. Mind you, I also recall not understanding this concept, shaking my head, and wandering off muttering something about the youth of today.

However, since the pandemic there has been a noticeable increase in the use of video communication. This is OK, replacing audio with video does help improve the richness of the interaction, but video can't fully address the need for face-to-face human communication and interaction.

As more people work from home we must look to extra-curricular activities to fill the void and to feed the desire for human communication. The role of the office will change, and it will cease to be solely a focus for work, but instead it will morph into a place where employees go to chat, interact, and communicate.

If you have a child in education, are starting your career, or wanting to keep ahead of others and AI, then you need to be able to communicate clearly, articulate fully, and provide unambiguous expectations.

The core skill required to be successful in a world of AI is the ability to communicate and articulate clearly. This applies not only to how humans interact with each other but also how we interact with technology itself. Communication skills are declining at the exact point in time that we need them to be improving. The scene is changing faster than ever before, and we need to change with it; those who can't change, won't change, or do not have the support or learning mechanisms to change will fall behind and risk becoming part of an unemployable subset of humanity. The only way to avoid this is to improve and develop our communication skills, both verbal and written. I will talk about how we attempt to address this complex challenge in Part 4.

Chapter 7 – Deep Engagement

Something that makes humans different from most other species on the planet is the ability to ponder, consider, evaluate, and set the little grey cells to work, figuring out how to deal with a complicated topic or scenario. This is referred to as deep engagement. Interacting with information in such a way that it leads to critical thought, emotional resonance, intellectual growth and more. You are reading this book; therefore, it is reasonable to assume that you are someone who likes deep engagement. Sadly, the vast majority of the people in the world are not like you.

In *1984*, thought is illegal, in *Brave New World* it is manipulated, and in *Fahrenheit 451* it has died out due to a lack of desire.

Let me expand a little further. *1984*'s depiction is very clear cut. Free thought and deep engagement are not permitted. If you attempt to think, or even think about thinking, you will be punished severely by the thought police. I find it interesting that Orwell chose to call out that thinking about thinking is as equally forbidden, as it suggests a far deeper, more unpleasant, level of control.

Brave New World has a different spin on it. The novel uses the conditioning and simple appeasement of society so that people have no desire to engage in anything deep and meaningful. Happiness and contentment, albeit superficial, are achieved through the consumption of Soma, a government issued drug that removes desire and calms the mind; issues disappear through the inducement of temporary sleep or sedation. Just 'pop a gramme' and the problem goes away.

Throughout *Brave New World*, intellect is portrayed as a threat to the control exerted by the World State, but as the book concludes you are presented with a twist where those of intellect are allowed to read and study as much as they like and wish. It is the desire of the elite to keep the masses in their place; kept ignorant, kept subjugated. Deep engagement in this world will take you great places, away from the populace, and introduce you to other like-minded people, but it is a high risk move to expose yourself considering the potential consequence of severe punishment.

Finally, we come to *Fahrenheit 451*, which again has a different tone. Here it is the people who have chosen ignorance. The people desire emotionally shallow, state provided content and programmes. Books have become largely obsolete. Technology has provided what the people wanted: summarised, simpler, and more immediately gratifying forms of information and entertainment. The resulting superficial knowledge and happiness created an environment where the elite could take advantage of society, apply censorship, and erode genuine connection without the people noticing. The decline in the desire for deep engagement is portrayed as a gradual process stemming from the populace itself and slowly 'drifting away' from reading and traditional forms of media.

There is a real indifference toward intellectual pursuit and an almost imperceivable erosion of intellectual growth. It is not simply a choice that has been made, but the beginning of a downward spiral. The weakening of intellectual muscles results in a population who are less likely to resist further intellectual degradation.

I believe we have started to see this intellectual degradation already, and *Fahrenheit 451* is the closest comparison from the three novels to what we see happening in society today. Not so much the state television or violence (although at the time of writing, things are looking unpredictable in certain countries) but from the increased desire for summarised content, shallow entertainment, and the growing lack of desire to engage at a deep level.

Deep engagement has been key to our success as humans for tens of thousands of years. We have used this skill to further our advantage over other species ever since we stepped away from being apes. We were, and are, curious about the environment around us, the universe, stars, planets, and why we exist. Scientists have spent centuries thinking about why things happen and creating problem solving machines. People read books on a staggering array of topics, fiction, fantasy, hard reads, and self-help. Children love exploring in nature and seeing what happens when you prod or poke something. Our brains have the capacity to learn new things, solve puzzles, remember huge quantities of information, and process data and visual clues at an astonishing rate. But to keep our brain thriving it needs to be exercised and challenged; it is an intrinsic part of our nature and without deep engagement we become passive receptacles.

Unfortunately, we are doing this less. Both children and adults are spending more time on a variety of screens and devices and are becoming those passive receptacles. For those who are avid book readers, you'll know that when you read you process the words, follow the storyline, and magnificently clear images will appear in your mind. The characters take form and become animated, new worlds are created, and the book comes to life. When you watch a movie or television show all those skills go unused; the characters and worlds are created for you, and you merely consume the content in front of your eyes. You become a passive receiver.

Future generations will no doubt blame AI for much of this decline; current ones too, I suspect. It is easy to put the blame at the door of AI, but this process started long before Gen AI took hold of the world. What is it about summarised and short-form content that attracts us to it? Is it laziness or efficiency? Why is society choosing to make this move?

In the three novels, as with real life, technologies are actively facilitating the consumption of, and constantly distracting the people with, superficial entertainment. Many of today's programmes are characterised by their simplified content which is purely there to keep your eyes entertained. The succession of images on screen is designed to produce distraction and fascination, but they go towards eliminating the opportunity for meaningful interaction and sustained thought.

The incessant bombardment of media makes it difficult for individuals to think or remember. The sheer speed and volume of abbreviated, short-form media counters our ability to execute deep and reflective thought, and therefore intellectual engagement becomes suppressed. It is a global problem and is very much more noticeable in the 'developed' world than in the 'emerging' world. Technology allows for rapid, short content to be delivered, and it enables the conditioning of our minds to prefer or even require it.

People are becoming addicted and conditioned; these technologies, devices, content and apps are all designed to bombard, distract, ping, beep, vibrate, notify, and ultimately hook you in.

When did you last see a couple or a group of people all sat in a bar, at dinner, or out in public, all looking at their own devices? When have you had a business conversation with someone who keeps checking their phone? When did you last see a child poking at their parent to get the attention away from their device? Even my dog hates me looking at mine!

These things are designed to demand your attention and tempt you into reading the message, or notification, immediately, all the time continuously breaking our attention, train of thought, or interrupting a conversation with a friend or colleague. People sit and scroll through thousands of images, videos, memes, and posts every day, and it is something that is easy to observe by the amount of time they leave it between putting down the device and picking it up again. This persistent distraction prevents any form of deep engagement. If you want deep engagement you need to close those devices and hide or turn off your phone.

We even see the decline of deep engagement in relation to the news headlines. These are now summarised to a single statement that has the sole aim of making you click through to the full article, where you are again bombarded with adverts and overly wordy text that is designed to string out your time on the page. Next time you see a news article on social media, have a think about it. If it really was aimed at providing you with an important news article, would it not just tell you what the story was about? Of course it would, but this is a tactic that has been around for decades, for example, newspapers that tell you to turn to page 6 for the full story. It is nothing new.

The worrying thing for me is that complex, geopolitical or domestic struggles are summarised into a ninety second read, because that is what we are being fed and conditioned to want. It is not uncommon to hear or see TL;DR (too long, didn't read) when the combination of the growing use of Gen AI tools and search engines has made it so easy to consume what you need without detail or cognitive effort.

If you need to know how to solve a problem on your boiler, you look it up. Suitable videos will be presented and, typically, AI will identify the part of the video you need. This replaces the process of challenging our brains to do something new, work something out, or understand a new concept, which is exactly the type of mental activity that embeds knowledge into our brain. Now we have gone direct to the answer without having to think about it or work it out, we haven't done anything to ingrain that information into our memory, and so the likelihood is that the next time it happens we will need to look it up again. Going direct to the answer is very useful and fast, but it must not become our sole avenue for learning.

We have moved towards a society of bite-sized nuggeteers.

If you apply that short-form approach to complex topics such as the growth of the Nazi party in the 1930s, the argument of trans and non-binary people, the history of Palestine and Israel, or India and Pakistan, then the complexity of the topics are so great that digesting a fraction of the story can be more damaging than knowing nothing. Garnering an incomplete picture on an immensely complex topic will do you no favours and is likely to end badly, but there are choices. I *could* spend a couple of weeks reading and viewing articles all about the rise of the Nazi party from different perspectives, I *could* watch documentaries on the topic, I *could* watch a short video or two, I *could* look at a social media platform, or I *could* ask Gen AI to summarise it for me and not bother reading or viewing anything at all. Every time I take a downward step, I lose another level of engagement.

Short-form content replacing deep engagement is a major contributor to the challenge we face regarding the decline of intellect and awareness within society. There are entire swathes of the global population who are now basing their thoughts and opinions on short, inadequate versions of a topic; and if those short versions are compounded with the reinforcement algorithms mentioned earlier then your view and understanding of the scenario or challenge will be incomplete and unbalanced. I cover filter bubbles and bias in more detail later.

Whilst writing this, I tried to determine the decline of book sales versus the rise in other entertainment. The short answer is that it is nigh on impossible to find any data. What would you compare it to? Gaming, streaming videos, messaging, browsing? Physical book sales seem to be holding steady as a market, so it feels like it is only possible to conclude that people do still read books, and if you are reading a book, then I don't believe that you are one of those people we need to worry about. If the global population is increasing rapidly and sales of books do not increase, then effectively it is decreasing.

It is the people who are preferring social media, Gen AI content, short-form, banal content that we need to keep in mind. Unfortunately, I do also believe this to be the majority, and in many cases, it is the younger generations who are and will be impacted the most. Books, reading, and learning with deep engagement is old fashioned and out of vogue.

Whilst not an expert in the field, I think it is fair to assume that the generations whose parents are already living off short-form content, with unverified sources, and who consume everyday banal entertainment, will pass this approach on to their children. Children take many of their cues from their parents after all.

Those who are adopting the use of Gen AI in everyday life need to tread carefully. These people will, I think, fall into a trap whereby they don't realise they are not engaging in a deep and meaningful way.

When these situations are combined, which is highly likely to happen, we will end up with a populace who are watching banal entertainment, whilst also scrolling through largely meaningless content, at the same time as being distracted by notifications, apps, or messaging friends. That means that none of those activities is getting full focus or attention, so all are distracting from each other, and all can therefore be considered shallow and superficial.

But the lack of deep engagement is far more widespread than this and goes even further. Watch almost any live event and you will see people watching the screen on their phone rather than immersing themselves in the real event. That might be because they are consuming other content or responding to notifications, or it might be because they are trying to capture the action for posterity. But by doing this they aren't committing the feel, the emotion, the action to their life experiences. They are choosing to offload that to technology. Yes, they can watch the videos back later and share them with others, but how often does that happen? It is more likely that it will be posted to social media, checked for likes, and promptly forgotten about. Live it!

If your child is in the school play, watch them be in the school play. If you are at a match, be in the stadium, the crowd won't vibrate your bones and fill you with emotion when the recording is played back. Live in the moment and breathe in the atmosphere. If you are watching it through a screen, you may as well be at home watching on television, or through your phone's tiny screen.

Deep engagement is not just attached to keeping up to date on politics and news or learning new topics, it also impacts the workplace. I cover the impact to business later, but deep engagement in the workplace can make work meaningful and rewarding. Without it, work is reduced to a set of tasks to execute.

In almost all lines of business, deep engagement nurtures your mental health, stretches your cognitive skills, and raises the morale of employees. As the workplace becomes more automated and relies more heavily on AI, deep engagement will start to decline there too. Employers and employees will need to find new ways of finding engagement for the new world and this leads to an entire chapter on reskilling your employees in readiness for new challenges.

Employees often work best when they feel valued and invested in. This is not about pay rises but about adding value to their lives and helping them learn new skills to develop themselves. When an employee is selected to go on a training course to learn a new skill, not necessarily a new product or a version upgrade, they come back enthused. I went on a change management course many years ago; it was more testing than any technical course I had been on, and I loved it. I know many people who feel the same, especially when learning new life skills. Don't underestimate the impact of boosting someone's mental engagement in this way. Remember we are curious creatures, and we like to learn, we like to be mentally stimulated, and it must be more frequent than once a year.

If we, as a society, lose deep engagement both at work and at home, then we have a major cognitive problem brewing. Gen AI tools are great, but if they are applied and allowed to take away our ability to think, then we essentially become robots or 'robota', a Czech word meaning forced labour or drudgery.

If we take away or lose deep cognitive engagement, then we will see a significant and further decline over the coming years as Gen AI embeds itself into our everyday lives. We are just starting to learn what these tools can do, and if in two years' time we have AI assistants making and manging appointments, writing solutions, engaging in the creation of client documents, telling us where we need to be and when, what route we should take to include sufficient EV charge points, summarising the news and political affairs, automatically looking at our health records, and suggesting and booking vacations; then where is our engagement?

I will look at the impact in more detail later, but we need to be very careful as we adopt these genuinely very clever technologies, that we don't become beholden to them. If we become passive receivers and no longer engage willingly, then we are exposed to misinformation and become complicit in the development of a society controlled by corporations and governments. If this happens then we take a step closer to a dystopia that is the crossover of the three novels.

If we lose the desire or ability to have deep engagement, we will become ignorant, shallow, ill informed, and easy to manipulate. Deep engagement is key to our success as a species, and without it we fall short of true satisfaction, meaning, and connection.

Chapter 8 – Critical Thinking

What's the difference between deep engagement and critical thinking? Deep engagement involves thorough immersion in information, resulting in a comprehensive understanding of the subject. Critical thinking is a higher order cognitive skill that employs comprehensive understanding to analyse, evaluate, and interpret the information so that a well-reasoned conclusion and judgment can be reached, and to solve problems. Deep engagement is the foundation for critical thinking and without this initial, thorough immersion, any analysis runs the risk of being flawed.

Our world, both socially and in business, is becoming increasingly complex. Critical thinking is, and will further become a vital skill for individuals, businesses, and societies over the coming years. As with deep engagement, critical thinking is under threat, which is not surprising when the two are so tightly linked. Search engines, access to the research of others, Gen AI, and non-generative AI can all be seen as contributors to the reduction in critical thinking; however, over the next few years we will see this particular skill become fundamental in both society and business, and will help to build some level of resistance against the spread of misinformation and manipulation.

Critical thinking, defined by experts as a 'higher order' cognitive skill, or higher order thinking skill, is something that goes beyond the ability to recall information. It is a set of interconnected skills that are based around the following: (caveat, there are several variations available.)

- **Analysis** is the ability to break down information, arguments, or problems into constituent parts to help understand the challenge.
- **Evaluation** is the assessment of the credibility, accuracy, and relevance of the information.
- **Inference** is the ability to draw logical conclusions and make reasoned judgements based on the information that has been analysed and evaluated.
- **Interpretation** is being able to recognise a problem, describe it objectively and clarify the meaning without bias.
- And finally, **explanation** is the articulation of thoughts in a clear manner and with the support of evidence.

Problem solving and decision making come as a result of the above steps.

Critical thinking is absolutely not the same as being critical, let's just make that one clear as it is something that gets confused all too often. The etymology of 'critical' goes back to the Greek word *kritḗs*, meaning 'judge'. A judgment can be positive, negative, or even a balanced assessment; being 'judged' typically comes with a negative connotation that is a psychological barrier when encouraging critical thinking in the workplace. Critical thinking is a term that is often misunderstood by both employers and employees.

It is widely acknowledged that there has been a noticeable decline in critical thinking skills within the workplace and educational establishments, but it is a skill that is in steep decline socially too.

NASA called it in the 1960s when they asked researcher George Land to find out why there was a dearth of critical thinkers coming out from colleges and universities. Land and his team devised and ran a series of tests against a group of children to test their critical thinking abilities. At the age of five, they found that there was a 98% chance that a child had the potential to be a genius. The test was repeated with the same children when they turned ten and fifteen and adjusted for their age. At the conclusion of the testing of the fifteen-year-olds, NASA pulled the plug on the testing. Why? Because at fifteen the 98% chance of genius had dropped to 12%. Land and his team continued to test at twenty years old, and the result was that by this age a child had a 2% chance of being a genius. It was education that was destroying critical thinking. I'll come back to education in a later chapter.

You don't need to dig too far to find many reports (Morson, 2020) that indicate a concern over the lack of critical thinking skills. Despite the acknowledged importance of these skills, they are in a state of further decline. In a very generalised and sweeping statement, those entering the workplace direct from education are great at memorising and recalling information but struggle in solving practical, real-world problems, and often confuse knowledge with intelligence.

Research has established a significant correlation between the frequent use of Gen AI tools and the decline in critical thinking abilities. 'Cognitive Offloading' as it is called is where cognitive tasks are delegated or 'offloaded' to external tools. The convenience offered by these tools, and I use them myself frequently, seems completely beneficial, but as we increasingly offload tasks to it, our cognitive functions that underpin critical thinking are exercised less frequently.

And so, we enter a negative cycle where we rely on the technology for perceived efficiency whilst inadvertently diminishing our cognitive ability, and so we rely more heavily on the technology, and so on. This reduction in our ability to think critically will lead to a greater perceived need for assistance from AI tools. We are walking towards a future where individuals are less capable of solving complex problems unaided.

In the UK, there has been research conducted by Ofcom (2025) which indicates that 40% of internet users do not possess the skills required to critically evaluate information, and that across all demographics there were challenges in applying this critical thinking to information presented to them in the online world. 87% of those surveyed expressed confidence in knowing about online information in 2024 and yet only 51% of search engine users could identify sponsored links. That's just a little bit; well, no, majorly worrying.

Adults often overestimate their media literacy skills, and when they do this and believe themselves to be proficient, they also reveal themselves to be less likely to seek out any help that could improve their skills. It creates a cognitive blind spot that makes them susceptible to misinformation; and yes, I cover misinformation later too. It is a significant concern, especially when the number of adults unable to identify a sponsored link is so high. If they can't identify a sponsored link, how are they expected to identify a manipulation of the truth? This leaves society open to all sorts of abuse, rogue beliefs, and manipulation from groups, corporations and governments, on a global scale.

The three novels are as clear on critical thought as they are on deep engagement. For each authority depicted critical thought is a firm no; it is not allowed. Each novel depicts critical thought as an absolute threat to society, or moreover to those in control over society. *Fahrenheit 451* portrays critical thinking as a route to dissent. Early in the book we are introduced to a character called Clarisse who is curious, who questions the way things are, and who seeks genuine connection. It is Clarisse who triggers the curiosity within the protagonist of the book, Guy, and although she is not in it for long, the impact of their meeting is the catalyst for the events that follow.

Brave New World moves away from the largely willingly ignorant populace to a model based more on appeasement. Critical thinking is deterred through the application of psychological conditioning, easy distraction and through the availability of the drug Soma. From birth, critical thought is treated as a bad thing, and so that is how it comes to be viewed by the people. When faced with a situation that requires critical thought the response is likely to be the consumption of more Soma. Critical thinking in *Brave New World* is unnecessary due to the manipulated contentment of the masses.

In *1984*, as you are coming to expect, critical thought is controlled through fear. The Party fights to eliminate critical thinking, or 'thoughtcrime' and through the actions of the ministry all words pertaining to independent thought have been removed from dictionaries and societal use. If the words don't exist, then you can't articulate your thoughts or ideas. This, combined with the surveillance of, and violence towards, those who do display signs of critical thought, gives the populace a good reason not to express any conceived ideas.

Three very different approaches but all with similar results; critical thinking is not allowed.

It is possible to see the decline in our ability to apply critical thinking. In education, in business, in society, in politics, and in the way that some demographics are starting to blindly accept what they are being told.

News and politics is one area that you can plainly see the impact of this. People are simply accepting information without question. 'I saw it on social media therefore it must be true', 'it must be true because so-and-so shared it', and so on. In the more developed countries around the world there is a real fight for misinformation with bodies, groups, organisations, political parties, and activists fighting to tell you what they want you to believe. They all compete for your screen time and attention; they rely on the 51% of adults who can't identify a sponsored link. They want to reach as many of the unquestioning followers as possible, regardless of whether it is true or not; and if is successfully consumed 'as fact' even better, they win.

I am going to pick on the US and UK, as recent events have seen huge sets of conflicting opinions on very serious matters. Again, it doesn't matter if it is true or not as it is about what those groups want you to buy in to, not what is fact. How many times have you seen things published on social media, declaring something to be true? And how many times do you go and validate that information from another source or viewpoint? There is a rapidly growing part of society that don't go and check. Why? Because it fits nicely to their existing beliefs or bias, so they are openly happy to accept the 'information'. We all make assumptions. I know that if I see news from certain publications or organisations, I will likely assume it to be false; but if it is a topic of interest or concern, I will go and research it further. You, as a reader of this book, are likely to do something similar, but if that story goes out, and the masses, who don't want to or can't apply critical thought to it, assume it to be true, then the group or person posting it gains momentum.

The impact on business is different. The business world is changing, and whilst technology can bring great benefits, we need a markedly different employee skill set to work with the new tools. The Confederation of Business Industry (CBI) report states that the UK alone will need 16 million people (Morson, 2020) to acquire critical thinking skills by 2030. That is not far away. Failure to address this will leave a cognitive gap in the workforce that will prevent the UK from evolving along with the technological advances. This is not isolated to the UK of course, it is a worldwide issue, and one that will bring with it a decline in competitive advantage and lead to well established businesses falling behind. Only those looking to embrace and develop critical thinking will gain an advantage over the competition.

Despite the concerns regarding its decline, critical thinking is widely considered to be something that can be learned and enhanced through sustained practice. This means that critical thinking can be taught within a classroom or business setting, and China has already announced that they will be teaching it as a mandatory subject in schools this year. If we do nothing, we will reach a point where other nations will leapfrog the complacent ones. We will have to see how this plays out, but I would not be surprised if we started to see this emerging in the next five to ten years.

There are some academics who believe that critical thinking, without reflection, can create a 'dark side' where negative analysis can inadvertently contribute to a dystopian world by undermining confidence and trust. If misused, it is thought that critical thinking can foster societal cynicism and distrust. But surely that is exactly what it should be doing: encouraging people to look with an element of cynicism and distrust. If we had more people looking at facts and information with that approach, we might be in a better position than we are now.

In education and business we need to start teaching how to think critically. Failure to do so will result in a real decline in our ability to live in a world with AI and it will lead to us filling in the gaps that technology is unable to deliver. Critical thinking will become another of the core skills required by humans.

Chapter 9 – Overload and Bubbles

Or to be more correct, 'Information Overload, Filter Bubbles, and Bias', but that was way too wordy.

What do I mean by each of these areas? Let's unpack the definitions first and then move on to the detail.

Information Overload has an official definition. 'When the volume of information an individual receives or is exposed to surpasses their inherent cognitive capacity to effectively accept, process, and respond to it.' Good huh? I'm pretty sure we have all felt like there is just too much information for our brains to process at one point or another. Information overload can foster negative or depressive thoughts, confusion, an inability to make decisions, stress you out, and can lead to mental exhaustion.

Filter Bubbles are when algorithms on websites, social media, and other online platforms selectively present information and content based on a user's past online activities and behaviours. Think click history, browsing patterns, search queries, etc. This results in the user being exposed to further information that aligns with their previous activity. I touched on this earlier; you are presented with content that aligns with your existing beliefs and likes rather than, and this is the bubble, being exposed to challenging alternatives or opposing and diverse viewpoints. You just get more of what you like. It is an echo chamber. There are other bubble types, but I don't think that we need to go down that particular rabbit hole just yet.

Bias on the other hand, we will explore at a high level as there are many different types; algorithmic, data, implicit, confirmation, social, stereotyping, and several more. When talking about bias in this chapter, it will be more about generic biases that can arise and how they manifest themselves. To dive into bias in any depth would require a book of its own.

All three shape the way our minds work with, and how we think about, information.

Let's begin with information overload. I run the risk of making myself sound old now, but back in the old days information came from a few distinct places; first it was books and newspapers, then we added radio to the mix, followed by television, and now we have information coming at us from all directions. Obviously, we haven't lost the other media, and we still have books, or at least I hope so or this little venture is doomed. Newspapers are around still, but not to the same scale as they were when many houses took a paper every day. Radio is still very popular, and is now supplemented with podcasts, and television has moved from a handful of terrestrial channels to hundreds of digital channels from all over the world. Satellite and internet-based services bring us almost any programme from almost any country, unless deliberately blocked for either commercial or political reasons.

Information still comes at us from all those directions, but now we have added social media platforms and communication platforms, including email and messaging or chat. When we walk past shops, we are advertised to; large public spaces frequently have big screens; and the apps we use each day fire adverts and information at us. And of course, in the workplace, we are also bombarded with information.

I am going to ignore direct human to human communication as a method for the exchange of information as I see that as falling out of the scope of this book.

Books, newspapers, and radio were the prevalent sources of information for decades; they were a gentler form of consumption compared to today's sources. If you wanted to know something you picked up a book or a newspaper, it wasn't thrust in your face or rammed down your throat. Likewise with radio, listening was originally something families did for entertainment and to keep up to date with the major news stories of the day. With radio it's up to you, you control when you choose to listen, and if you want to stop you can; just turn it off.

Modern technologies and apps push information at us. It is hard to carry your device around with you and escape the onslaught. Our typical day might consist of being woken up by some music, and that's nice, you may hear the day's headlines, and that is OK too but from there on in, until you go to sleep, you are pounded left, right, and centre with useful information, information that companies think might be useful but that isn't, information on what your friends are doing, information on products, on services, information on human rights and campaigns to prevent injustice, on what shoes are in fashion, where you can buy things cheaply, misinformation, lies, and so on; and let's not forget being hounded by work notifications too.

We are receiving so much new information during our waking hours while also catching up on what happened during our sleeping hours, that we risk spending most of our days just consuming information, not having the time to filter it for accuracy, truthfulness, relevance, or importance.

Information has changed from being a desirable thing that we chose to consume, to a force-fed stream, cleverly designed and architected and pushed to us at all hours of the day. Most people seem to tolerate this quite happily, but in the workplace, it is often not something that you can choose to put down, turn off or ignore. Many workplaces are now following suit with emails, intranet notifications and feeds, collaboration notifications, planner tools chasing your deadlines, project tools assigning tasks to you, chats, and messages. Even worse than this, and a personal hate of mine, is having access to work apps on personal devices. The pressure of the workplace, combined with a common fear of being seen as under-performing if you don't respond at all hours. It leads to a counterproductive way of working and living. It's not at all healthy, a subject I'll explore later.

Filter bubbles also compound information overload. Not only is all this information being shoved in my face, but my perspectives are being narrowed due to the similarity of the information being shoved at me. We've all seen it in action; if I buy an ink cartridge from a website, it is most likely that for the next few days all I will see is offers on where to buy ink cartridges from. Which, of course, is nonsense, dare I say not very (Artificially) Intelligent, as I've just bought one, so won't need another for a while. If I support right-wing groups and newsfeeds, then I will get more of the same. (For balance, it's the same on the other side.) When filter bubbles combine with the volume of information, you get a barrage of like-minded content that is akin to brainwashing. This is an underappreciated danger.

For us to be open minded, we need a balance of information and perspectives, but that is not what technology is currently designed to give us. Why is this? Simple, it is not in the service or app provider's interest. You are the product; you are the target. An app creator is fighting for screentime, attention and engagement. Why would they then show you stuff that you have shown no interest in? They want to show you more stuff that is in your arc of interest. There is no moral high ground here, no ethics in play; just more of what they know you like and what you have engaged with, to make you spend more time on their platform/app and probably see more ads, allowing them to charge the advertisers more as they can show there's been more eyeballs for longer consuming their content. Filter bubbles have a lot to answer for as this is where it starts to impact society. Take the political scene, and I am not going to take any sides, but rest assured I have strong views about looking out for our fellow humans. When national, political, and other activists use technology to feed social media streams, and you choose to interact with or like that content, then you are going to be fed additional content along that line. Remember that we have just talked about the decline of critical thinking and deep engagement, so the responsible thing to do is to look at your feed and wonder why you are only getting information that is aligning to your views and thoughts.

Someone who has strong political right-wing views, will continue to live in a social media feed of pro-right-wing, anti-left-wing content, and that will continue unless something changes in the technology, governance, or the minds of the populace. Perversely, if you are right-wing and decide to explore left-wing politics out of sheer curiosity, then be prepared for more left-wing views to be dropped in front of your eyes.

Lastly, and closely tied to filter bubbles, is bias. Whereas filter bubbles are created through technology and cause your scope of perspective to be narrowed, bias is an inherent human trait and influences our judgement and decisions. Bias is how we think, and filter bubbles are what we are shown. Filter bubbles reinforce our biases.

Bias, however, also raises its virtual head in the world of AI, and it is a very important thing to be aware of. Humans have both conscious and unconscious biases; confirmation, affinity, political, and gender bias all feature. In fact, we can, and do, have biases about almost anything.

Bias becomes particularly important when interacting with AI. Gen AI in particular is, at the time of writing, still open to showing us pre-existing biases like doctors being male and nurses being female. This is primarily because AI has been trained on all the available information it can find, including those with existing and historical biases. This will change over time as it learns and develops and as we correct it, but it is also open to being fed our own subconscious biases. Back to the political scene: if I have a political bias towards the left or right, the language I use to create a prompt or interaction can influence the output and response that I get. Even phrases that may seem inconsequential play a part. A phrase like 'for *his* approval' is enough to vary a response. We need to be far more mindful of the use of our chosen words.

Try asking a Gen AI tool or assistant to review your prompts and content for any forms of bias including gender, race, faith, or social, and it will typically do a reasonable job. It doesn't need to be complicated, a simple '*Please review this text, and help me identify any bias in the language I have used and provide suggestions for alternative wording.*' This is something I do regularly with important comms and documents, and it has correctly identified gender normalisation that I have missed. I wouldn't be surprised if we saw email services include the ability to review content for bias before it is released to the receiving email system, or documents being automatically checked before being released. The technology exists already, but I suspect it will become part of the standard solutions in due course.

Why are information overload, bubbles, and bias important? When you combine them together, they create a broken environment for us to live and work in. Nobody likes being nagged, but we willingly allow ourselves to be nagged by technology. If it was a person treating us like that, we'd get fed up with them very quickly. We get nagged, reminded, notified, messaged, both, one-to-one and in groups. We see a narrow viewpoint that only goes to serve our existing interests in the name of the fight for screentime and attention. We are bombarded by adverts in the middle of videos, in apps, on television, before you can stream content, and when trying to read an article. We are fed misinformation, manipulation and lies; we deal with more information than experienced by any previous generation, and we are starting to lack the cognitive skills or capacity to deal with it effectively.

This is going to lead to a general burnout of society and a growing crisis around mental health. Technology has a huge part to play here, there can be no doubt, but we can't put the blame wholly on technology. *The Rise of the Humans* by Dave Coplin (Coplin, 2014) is a good short read which says, in summary, that we have the choice to consume or not to consume. We have the right to be notified or not. We have the right to disconnect, but for whatever reason most of us choose not to. Is it the fear of missing out, the desire to feel needed, and notifications provide us with that comfort? Or is it more like an addiction? Perhaps there is something more sinister at work, such as a corporate attempt to rewire our brains? I don't know, I am not a psychologist, but something is appealing to our nature.

In the three novels, information overload, filter bubbles, and bias are used to good effect. *1984* does not rely heavily on information overload, but the systematic feeding of information is a key element as the party lines are continually pumped out. It is a one-way feed of propaganda, with filter bubbles and bias used to great effect.

In *Brave New World* and *Fahrenheit 451*, information overload is used to drive contentment through distraction, something that I will argue is already happening in our world. Whilst the information we are subject to today is of a far broader spectrum, the principle of distraction and superficial, shallow content resonates strongly.

Bias is, of course, a potent tool in the dystopian novel. These biases are far from sub-conscious; they are deliberately manufactured by those in power to shape and control the masses. They are fed systematically through media, the telescreens, and reinforced through fear.

In our world today this is largely driven by commerce and the desire to hook you in, but I venture to say that there is a far darker side to its use. Consider how much easier it would make things for many governments around the world if they had a populace that lacked curiosity, were passive, and who went along with whatever they were being told. If I look around at the geopolitical scene, I see long-established authoritarian regimes using these very techniques; but now I see similar but less established happenings in 'developed' nations around the world, including the UK and USA.

It is something that is remarkably easy to spot if you have your head screwed on right. There does seem to be an element of the Dunning-Kruger effect in play where those who believe themselves to be competent when dealing with online information, filter bubbles and bias, actually lack the skills to support that claim, and because they lack the skills to support the claim, they are unable to see they are not as competent as they portray. Recall the statistic I mentioned earlier where 87% of people expressed confidence in knowing about online information and yet only 51% of search engine users could identify sponsored links! That is the effect in action.

I think it unlikely that there will be any kind of downturn in information overload. Trying to change the minds of the hundreds of thousands, if not millions of commercial organisations actively using these mechanisms seems like a task that would be almost impossible and would take a very long time to achieve. Pushback is more likely to be triggered by an event that causes resentment or hurt. Asking these businesses to willingly change their approach because the people are receiving too much information is not going to float.

There is an additional, compound issue here too. The number of posts and media shared by an individual organisation might not be the problem, but when *you* are following hundreds of pages, groups, and people, each posting a reasonable amount, you are contributing to information overload, not them. I think the reversal of information overload is only really going to be achieved by individuals themselves disconnecting, unfollowing, and being more selective about what information they choose to receive.

Filter bubbles is a more intriguing topic. This is something that could potentially be resolved by technology. If a Filter Bubble or echo chamber is the phenomenon where you are shown further content that aligns with your existing beliefs or interests, it would be comparatively easy to get the technology to suggest a wider or opposing set of views. The challenge with this would be that, as mentioned, most social media platforms look at what you like. They are fighting for screentime, attention, and engagement, so when you are asked if you would like to see more of this kind of content, if you say no, they will just surface the next topic. What might be more manageable for politics, etc., is to remove the algorithmic element and just show people things from a range of angles. Maybe this is something that could apply to a certain range of topics? How about gender, race, war, religion? The main challenge here is that once more we would be asking commercial organisations, who make money from collecting data about you and who sell that data on as intelligence, to essentially stop collecting data. So, I can't see that one happening either. That is only going to be resolved by individuals learning to look at a topic, apply critical thinking, and go looking for alternative viewpoints. This is much more of a societal thinking fix. I might not hold my breath on that one either, not just yet.

Finally, bias is something that is engrained into us from infancy. We will typically be exposed to our parents' and local societal biases; these are the foundational biases that we have as we develop from a child to an adult. We eventually reach our own conclusions and form new biases, drop others, and hopefully try to be a balanced human being. We need to teach people from infancy right the way through to adulthood how to manage bias, how to identify it, how to address it in ourselves, and how to tackle others about their biases. We will never create a uniform set of biases where everyone agrees and I wouldn't want that, life would be very dull, but on major topics I would like to see people at least being able to identify biases and to challenge them. That is half the battle we face. There are enormous swathes of the world's population who go along with their political view because they were brought up as Conservative, Labour, or Lib Dem (Republican or Democrat for those who are stateside), etc., and when questioned about why they vote that way they are rarely able to articulate their choices based on any discernible policies.

We are surrounded by information overload, filter bubbles and biases; is there a technical fix? No. Again the responsibility falls, for now, back on to the shoulders of individuals. It is therefore necessary to wake people up to the large amount of sleepwalking that is taking place.

Chapter 10 – Truth Under Siege

Now we have established that deep engagement is on the slide, that critical thinking is a dying skill, and that we are living in a world where we are on the receiving end of a barrage of information that is (a) targeted at us and (b) reinforces our biases and pre existing thinking, we can move on to Truth.

The truth is that the Truth is under siege. It is being neglected by us through the impact of information overload, filter bubbles, and bias, but it is also under massive pressure just to be seen. The staggering increase in content that is either a manipulation of the truth or an outright lie, combined with our lack of interest in fact checking, makes it easy to distort the true picture.

I'm going to start with an incredibly obvious statement. The truth is important. Truth is founded in factual information and evidence. If we are presented with facts and evidence we are able to draw conclusions that have been based on something real.

A prime example of this is Brexit; the UK deciding whether or not to leave the European Union. Apart from the prime failing of Brexit, which was that a very complicated matter was boiled down to a yes/no question, it was something that had never been undertaken before. There was no precedent, no past example, no clue of what might happen; no country had ever left before, so the implications were completely unknown. Both campaigns rallied hard, both campaigns made information up, both pitched ideas on how good or bad it might be, both played on fear, and both lied. Arguably, one side did a better job of this than the other, but the reality was that both campaigns made things up and there was hardly a truth in sight. If you don't have facts and evidence, how can you make an informed judgement or decision? This led to campaigns of fear, made up statistics, and supposition that suited each campaign's narrative. All forms of media were blurting out all kinds of nonsense, and social media led the charge. Technology was used to flood feeds with emotive content.

The challenge today is that truth and facts seem to count for less than they used to. Why is that? Has the truth become less valuable; less important? Highly unlikely. I want to explore a few areas, and I am going to start with those who want to, and are, publishing the truth.

For those people, organisations, and businesses around the world who are using technology to publish genuine and truthful content, well, I wish you all the best in your fight to gain attention. Even those with the most noble of intentions like charities and social welfare organisations are trying to get their stories, and the truth, noticed. You could have the best product or service, be telling the most compelling, amazing story, even giving people the best news in the world, but you will always be fighting against the volume of lies, manipulation, and sensationalist content that is so engaging to the populace these days.

Bad news and scandals have always travelled faster than good news, that has been understood for many years. The reason behind it is open to great discussion and debate. Theories range from the evolutionary need to know of danger quickly, to studies that confirm that negative news induces a state of heightened physiological arousal and attentiveness. Sounds a bit dodgy to me, but I guess it would explain quite a few things about society.

The other challenge that the genuine publishers have is the impact that the lack of deep engagement and critical thinking and the prevalence of filter bubbles prevents people spotting falsehoods and misinformation and blinds them to the truth. Truthful posts and real news get buried in the melee of noise and nonsense, and so the impact is lost. It is a bum deal for those wanting to use the platforms for good.

For those who deliberately go out to publish lies and misinformation, social media is a dream medium. If I tell lies in a UK newspaper, I will be instructed to issue an apology by the regulator. Don't get me started on how these apologies are dealt with or we will be here a long time, but there is governance and recourse for printing lies and misinformation. The same applies to television. Social media on the hand has little to no regulation. It was never designed to be a source of news; it was there to connect friends and like-minded people, hence the label 'social'. The percentage of adults consuming news in the UK is 96%, online consumption of the news is around 71%, but 52% garner their 'news' from social media (Ofcom, 2024). Of course, that number will vary depending on where you live and your source of information, and I don't want to get into the debatable detail here, but it is significantly high whichever source you look at.

This number increases dramatically to 88% for sixteen- to twenty-four-year-olds. The idea of providing these numbers is not to call out any generational shift, but to highlight that the shift of news consumption from TV to social media is both significant and unlikely to regress.

Consumers of social media news content do seem to be aware that accuracy is lower, and that manipulation and lies are more prolific, but given that we have already seen statistics about the inability to identify sponsored links I'm not sure I'm going to put my faith in their ability to correctly identify 'fake news'.

'Fake news' is a term I thoroughly detest. It has become such a dreadful and overused term and is used to cover all sorts of areas with its most famous claimant using it as some sort of valid argument. A valid argument would surface counter evidence, but no, it is just claimed to be fake, and alarmingly this seems to be sufficient for many. The identification of something being genuinely fake has become devalued. If it is true and gets called fake it is viewed by many as fake, and if it is fake and it gets called out as fake, it makes no odds as to whether there was any element of truth there in the first place.

Another concerning factor in the battle for truth is those people delivering 'slight mistruths' (Yes, I have made that term up, but I couldn't think of anything better suited.) My definition of a slight mistruth is where you present a story that is almost entirely credible but change some of the information or facts to suit your narrative. The best fantasy stories have just enough real-world connection to make them more believable or possible. This type of manipulation is far harder to spot for an already struggling audience as it allows the person posting the information to 'tweak' the truth. This has been done for decades, but the spread and speed of social media means that it will probably never be called out as a lie, and certainly not in a timely manner. The seed is sown, the content is widely spread, and the deed is done.

To confuse matters further still we have to consider sloppy reporting and article creation. In English, there is a big difference between 'I like cooking my family and pets' and 'I like cooking, my family, and pets'. One portrays a psychopath and the other a wholesome person. Even a cursory glance through social media will show that the lack of correct grammar can change the meaning of a sentence dramatically. Headlines and articles are becoming increasingly inaccurate due to poor standards of written English.

A far darker area of misinformation in the battle for Truth is the political and geopolitical scene. It is very difficult to get to the truth of what happens in this area; from an outsider's perspective, regardless of the medium, it appears to be a melting pot of lies, misinformation, and manipulation.

Political parties having the ability and platform to 'speak' directly to the populace is something I agree with, but as we have seen, algorithms can turn this into a Filter Bubble. What if I wanted to play dirty in my political career or race to the premiership? It would be very easy for me or my team to put out a post saying that my rival was financially tied to a drugs cartel and is under investigation for criminal activities, or has been subject to a public enquiry into insider trading, or that they have vested interests in private medical companies when they are responsible for the public health services. Do I have to make that statement truthful and factual? Not for it to make an impact. The post would be seen by thousands of people because I have paid for it to be pushed out to a chosen demographic that meets my narrative. If anyone were to challenge the misinformation I might remove the post, but by then the damage is done. I have succeeded; all those people have seen the information that my rival is a crook. Will they look to check the information? Maybe, but even so it is likely to seep into the subconscious as 'accepted content that has been read'.

Countries, states, and parties all around the world now play these games. Russia and China always appear at the top of the list as being seen to influence voting in elections outside of their borders, but they are by no means alone. AI powered tools and bots post content all over social media, and with little to no regulation they can influence the minds of many in how they vote.

Organised misinformation campaigns are often state-backed or funded by private corporations with the goal of manipulation, creating division, and undermining democracy. The speed that these organised campaigns can operate is eye-watering and very difficult, if not impossible, to counter effectively.

There is an old saying, 'follow the money'. Look at who stands to gain. If political party A can discredit a candidate from party B, bingo, you have power.

'Rage Bait' is posted on social media by supporter organisations and false identities to make completely outrageous claims, claims that are far from the truth and near impossible to believe. They are placed to start a torrent of counter comments, noise, and distraction. 'Politician cheered on by party supporters for beating a chicken to death at child's party' or other such nonsense. One recent post was that the UK 'loved Donald Trump so much' that we wanted him to 'become our Prime Minister'; err, nope, that is just distraction. And even a single post like that can be further manipulated and amplified: 'Trump for PM, people say' will attract far more attention than 'One person on Twitter posted this' and become accepted as true as described above.

Rage bait serves a purpose in distracting and inflaming but being able to discredit someone is powerful. If a fossil fuel energy company dislikes the environmental policy from party A, it might look to support party B, or discredit A, or both. The powers behind the fossil fuel industry might engage in a campaign to discredit Party A's policy which recommends an increase in mining of minerals for battery production. 'Look at the scars left on the planet from sourcing additional materials for electric vehicle batteries.' We could debate whether the scars left by mining materials for electric cars are any better or worse than those left by traditional power forms, it is sort of a dystopian destruction of the planet, but that is not in scope of this book. What is important is that we understand the motive: electric vehicle sales are eating into the fossil fuel industry's profits, so they play on Party A's policy being damaging to the environment. It has nothing to do with being eco-friendly, no, the fossil fuel industry is protecting its financial interests, not the interest of the planet.

The same principle can be applied to many things.

Wealthy people will nearly always vote for tax cuts and efficiencies, regardless of the party in question. Private medical companies will always have bosses that vote for the increased privatisation of national medical services. When you read something, anything, ask yourself 'who benefits from this?'

One thing that crossed my mind whist writing this was 'is Truth dying?' I don't think it is, the truth can't die, it is what happens or happened, and so there is hope. What is happening is that the truth is being buried under all the other nonsense that is being fed to us. Misinformation is very much on the rise and will continue to be for many years until there is a smart way to flag it. Maybe AI can help, after all it is being used to create the mess, so maybe it can be used to help clear it up too?

In *1984*, Big Brother declares as part of its manifesto that there will be no reduction in the chocolate rations for the people. That promise is subsequently broken, and the ration is reduced from 30g to 20g. The book says, 'It appeared that there had even been demonstrations to thank Big Brother for raising the chocolate ration to twenty grammes a week. And only yesterday, he [Winston, the protagonist] reflected, it had been announced that the ration was to be REDUCED to twenty grammes a week. Was it possible that they could swallow that, after only twenty-four hours? Yes, they swallowed it.'

At around the same time as reading that part of *1984*, I heard an announcement from the UK government that was far too close in tone for comfort. At this point I berate myself for not making a note of what it was, because I can't remember for the life of me, but it felt just like that. Maybe this is where we are with our battle for truth. Are we starting to see blind denial and contradiction being accepted? Not if I have anything to do with it, no. It is very hard to express how important the truth is; we spend decades telling our kids not to lie, and yet it seems to be becoming a socially acceptable part of life, so long as it helps you get what you want.

Smaller groups who have found it difficult to find a public voice now have access to the same stage as corporates and governments. They now have the reach of social media to share their content and their objections. If something is deemed by them to be offensive, they have a global platform on which to voice it. Controversial views are not a bad thing: without it our world would be a bland, appeasing, and non-confrontational environment where tough topics were given no consideration in case someone took offence. But to avoid confrontation many feel that self-censorship is better than risking debate or confrontation.

Truth is key. We all have to take a role in protecting it and calling out lies, mistruths, and the rampant flow of manipulated information. Until better practical and effective mechanisms are introduced, this one remains on us. Fact check, question, and discredit the lies. Social media has such a potential for the positive but is easily turned into a toxic space.

Chapter 11 – The Battle for Data

We are at a critical point in time when it comes to data. Data and information have become the primary battleground in the modern world. *1984*, *Brave New World*, and *Fahrenheit 451* all call this out. Data is gold.

Data falls into two areas in my thinking: data within the corporate environment, and data that is collected about us. In the corporate arena, data is an extremely powerful tool; it often hides hugely valuable information, trends and statistics. Any organisation that underestimates the value of information held in their data is missing a trick. However, I want to focus on the data that is collected and being held about us, how that is incredibly valuable to businesses, and how it can be used against us.

The scale of personal data collection is huge, and the relationship between big data companies and governments is becoming questionable. Corporations have long held lots of data on clients, spending patterns, lifestyles, etc., but the lines between corporate and government have become blurred due to outsourcing contracts. I'm not accusing anyone of having directly broken the law, but I am raising a question about who should have access to such powerful information. Information and data have emerged as the main battleground in the modern world. Data, in all forms, is used to drive economic growth, shape political discourse, and influence society. Surveillance has transcended governmental mandates to become largely driven by big tech firms.

Today's equivalents of Orwell's telescreens are modern TVs, smartphones, laptops and tablets that are found throughout public and private spaces. These things bother me far more than security cameras. They constantly collect data on our activities, conversations, and locations. Whilst we don't like the idea of being monitored and surveyed by our governments, we do openly invite, embrace, and welcome these technologies and the big tech firms into our lives and homes. I'm no different to anyone else in that sense. In general, we are becoming increasingly aware that these devices are perpetually observing us. But what are they observing? I will cover that in a moment.

This widespread acceptance of surveillance into our lives has seen us shift from a general distrust and paranoia about being monitored, to willingly carrying telescreens around with us and inviting active, listening devices like smart speakers into our homes. This makes resistance to surveillance far more difficult as the mechanisms being used are seamlessly integrated into technologies and services that we desire and crave. There is no need for *1984*-style oppression; we are willing and compliant.

Modern society exhibits striking parallels to the three novels. Our obsession with media and the endless, meaningless stream of entertainment is very much established, but with one major difference; the big media screens are now millions of tiny screens. The constant stream of endless content, banal entertainment and noise in our personalised feeds draw parallels with the government issued drug, Soma. Just as Huxley's Soma chemically suppresses discomfort, technology creates a comfortable reality for us by constantly feeding us stuff that makes us happy or keeps us entertained.

Companies collect data of all sorts, and the scale of data captured and consumed globally is now reaching volumes that we could not have imagined twenty years ago. In 2024, the reported volume of data, globally, stood at 149ZB (Bartley, 2025) where a Zettabyte is 1,000,000,000 Terabytes, and it is expected to reach 181ZB by the end of 2025. To put that in context for us older folk, you would need a staggering 31.7 trillion (31,700,000,000,000) DVDs or 106 quadrillion (106,000,000,000,000,000) old school 1.44MB floppy disks to store 2024's data.

It is estimated that 90% of this data has been collected and created in the past two years, since Gen AI was launched to the public. The volume of stored data is doubling approximately every four years.

Individuals often don't seem to understand or know how to control their digital footprint. This is not a criticism of those individuals, but it does open a wide opportunity for the big tech firms. It is now about who possesses the capability to process, analyse, and extract value from that data; the ability to make sense of the data becomes the ultimate determinant of power.

The type of personal data collected can be broadly categorised into four main types.

- **Personal Data**: This is identity-related information, such as names, gender, National Insurance and Social Security numbers, etc., alongside device-related information like IP addresses and device IDs. This data is primarily collected to classify users into different demographics, and is used for advertising, audience interaction, and tailoring content to a target audience.
- **Usage Data**: This tracks and records user interactions with websites, text messages, emails, advertisements, and other online activities. This data is used to build accurate consumer profiles which are then used to determine and predict appropriate content, including adverts, engagement levels, and how long that engagement lasts.
- **Behavioural Data**: This qualitative data includes purchase histories, repeat actions, time spent on platforms, and navigation patterns. It is used to identify favourite purchases and interactions. It allows similar content or products to be suggested effectively.
- **Attitudinal Data**: Companies use this to measure brand and customer experiences. Consumer satisfaction, product desirability, and purchase decisions are all captured and used by marketing agencies as direct consumer research and analysis.

Companies like Google mine data. Google tracks and analyses everything Google-related; emails, call history, locations, searches, and browsing preferences, even when you are in an incognito browsing session. Meta (Facebook and Instagram) collects phone numbers, private messages, public comments, and metadata from photos and videos (things like geolocation etc.). Amazon stores a wide range of user data points, including phone numbers, credit card information, usernames, passwords, search terms, buying history, and items that are 'frequently bought together'. X (formerly Twitter) has various, quite insidious ways of gathering sensitive user data which they achieve by partnering with other applications, and Apple offers users more privacy controls, but still mines huge amounts of user data for its iOS-based advertising and App Store customisation.

They are all at it; every big tech company out there is doing it. Read the Terms and Conditions properly one day. Microsoft, Google, Apple, Samsung, Huawei; yep, all of them. If you read the Terms and Conditions, you will find some very interesting points, especially when applied to the Gen AI tools. You think your data is private? Well, unless you built your own Large Language Model (LLM), or Small Language Model (SLM), then unlikely.

But this data capture goes much deeper than simple demographics; it captures intricate details of the usage, behaviour and attitudes exhibited by the user; how they think, what they desire, and aims to predict what their next actions might be. This deeper version of profiling can be more comprehensive and predictable than the conscious self-awareness of the user. Deeply personal information, private messages, and saved photos are also captured and go towards blurring the line between your chosen public interactions and your intimate personal life. This level of detail can be used to advertise to you, yes, but it is also used for manipulation, as frequently seen in targeted political content. Whilst we may think our security settings are 'locked down' from others, we are willingly opening our personal lives to the big tech firms, to allow them to constantly optimise their commercial or political assault on us.

Companies collect information in all sorts of ways. Cookies, for example, are everywhere. How many times each day do you click a message about accepting or rejecting cookies, or accepting essential cookies and rejecting non-essential, or just being asked to manage your options? Regardless of whether you accept or reject the additional ones, cookies facilitate websites that you use to be personalised ('Welcome back, Pete') and to maintain your user login state. Those little things that go towards making your experience that bit nicer, a little slicker... whilst also tracking your access to the site, noting the pages you view, and any activity. It's not all they do: when you download applications, check in on social media platforms, and take photos, location information is automatically stored. GPS tracking and the capture of geolocation information is a bit more widespread that most realise. Many devices now ask if you want to share your location information or not, so if you are using a navigation solution, or searching what's nearby; great, go for it, but if you are buying perfume maybe they don't need to know where you are.

This concept of tracking where you are is not limited to GPS. Wi-Fi, particularly in stores, hotels, coffee shops, and expos, etc., ask you to share your information in exchange for free internet access, and we do, quite happily. Our need to be connected is so great we willingly hand over this information. Someone has even adapted Maslow's hierarchy of needs to show internet access as being more fundamental than our need for air, water, food and shelter, and people do act as if that were the case.

Someone offering free internet access not only collects the information you provide but will likely track your movements in their space. This data can verify physical visits, and at larger venues track the path you take, providing enough data to allow the venue owner to show real footfall and charge premium rates for certain pitches. It shows how long you are there, where you stop, and what websites you might visit while connected; all this information is then used to make changes to shop layouts and dictate where special offers are best placed. You might think store layouts are about being pretty and welcoming, but there is no point in it looking nice if people don't spend money, and so tracking movement is the primary function. It is the same principle as supermarkets moving their stock around periodically; it makes you stay in the store longer and walk around more, even if it is frustrating.

These tactics are often supported by the use of loyalty or reward cards. It's nice that the store is giving you something back for shopping regularly with them, isn't it? No, of course it's not. Remember to follow the money: it is an easy mechanism for them to gain more information about you and your purchasing habits, preferences, which promotions work for you, and what your favourite day to shop is. But that is

OK, because after spending £1000 with them you will have enough for a free coffee.

And there's more; licence plate images and location data show where your car was and what direction you were heading in. Different countries have different laws on this, but it can reveal movements and behavioural patterns. Facial recognition is on the rise too, again with differing laws, but a growing number of businesses are using this to recognise customers, greet them by name, amend advertising, and target offers based on what they know about buying habits.

While some of these methods are widely known and accepted, the trend is moving towards the less visible and more insidious techniques. It is sophisticated and pervasive and goes far beyond online interactions, often without explicit consent.

We are now subject to comprehensive and continuous surveillance that people are largely unaware of. Even public spaces are essentially now data collection zones, and your everyday activities are now just data points. This level of tracking and datapoint collection outstrips anything Orwell, Huxley, and Bradbury could perceive, and this collection of data about individuals raises additional questions about the security of that data. Is the data that is held about you secure?

The short answer is probably yes; hackers are getting increasingly more sophisticated and the weakest link in any security chain is the human one. It is typically easier to exploit the human and work your way in than it is to crack through layers of security. The question is not whether your data is secure but if the use of that data is legally protected and the ethics of the company holding it.

The big data and big tech firms are not likely to openly flout the law, but they will exploit every little loophole that they can if it can be monetarised. If they collect data about you, are they then allowed to sell it? Or maybe share it with a third-party organisation? And what about within different geographies? Are they allowed to pass data from Europe to another part of the world?

Data, in general terms, is subject to handling regulations. In Europe that is the General Data Protection Regulations (GDPR). This defines how data is to be stored, secured and governed, and breaching it can carry hefty fines; a maximum of €40 million or 4% of the company's annual global turnover. Similar regulations are to be found all around the world, which is all well and good, but if the data is protected under regulation, it can still be exploited ethically if the information that can be determined from it proves to be of value.

Ambiguity creates loopholes and makes the enforcement of privacy regulations difficult. It undermines the effectiveness of data privacy laws and allows companies to exploit these areas. Individuals may well believe their data is protected; often it's not. Regulating a rapidly changing digital landscape with traditional legal frameworks leads to a data battleground.

National security is another interesting area when it comes to data. Government agencies worldwide routinely request user information from tech companies. For now, major technology companies, including Google and Meta, publish 'transparency reports' that detail the number and type of requests they receive and from which government agency, and they are careful to point out that each request is reviewed to ensure it satisfies 'applicable laws'. It is not uncommon for these requests to be questioned, challenged, or refused.

Most government agencies will actively engage with the private sector to share information, people, processes, technologies, innovations, and ideas with the claimed benefit of strengthening national security. The question then arises 'How much do you trust your government?' Please excuse me for a moment whilst I pick myself up off the floor from laughing too much. Where do we start with answering that? Do I trust the UK government? Nope. I suggest we leave that there.

Public and private collaborations are, in theory, OK if it results in efficient processes, so long as any sensitive pieces of information remain protected. But the relationships between governments and private firms are often treated with a level of secrecy, as if the populace wouldn't like the idea of it. There are organisations that are far too close to our governments, certainly in the USA and UK. This is where I have grave concerns and can see clear parallels between the dystopian novels and today's world. Giving public data to potentially unethical big data firms feels like lining ourselves up for manipulation and surveillance. This goes way beyond simple government requests for data; it involves partnerships and mutual information sharing. The huge amount of data collected is not merely a commercial asset but is very much a strategic national asset, and that makes tech companies an extension of national intelligence.

Private data becoming a 'resource' for big data firms, in the name of national security, feels wrong. I have significant concerns about civil liberties, corporate practice, and democratic oversight. Individuals, educated on the topic or not, expect a certain level of privacy and protection, and this trust will be significantly eroded if it is done without public knowledge or consent. This data battleground and the desire for absolute power is a major theme that runs through nearly all dystopian depictions.

The dystopian novels painted a picture around the control of information. In the real world this has evolved into a more complex version where corporate data collection, driven by profit, is being integrated with government surveillance.

Historically, surveillance has been a government function requiring specific legal justification. Today, surveillance is commoditised and privatised, and the data is seen as a valuable resource that governments and businesses can access.

This is the beginning of a surveillance economy. It shifts the burden of protection from the government to the individual and creates powerful tech companies whose business models are based on collecting data about you.

You are being monitored and tracked far more than you know. This surveillance comes in a multitude of forms, some overt, some insidious and sneaky. The data collected needs to be handled carefully and subjected to great regulation and governance. Politically there needs to be greater clarity between public and private interactions when such personal data is in play.

Chapter 12 – The Loss of Wisdom

It feels rather sad to write this, but wisdom is very much on the decline. Wisdom is defined as 'the ability to use your knowledge and experience to make good decisions and judgments'.

Chapter over? No... wisdom is critical to our future, but yes, it, like deep engagement, critical thinking and other things mentioned in previous chapters, is on the decline. This book is starting to sound all doom and gloom, but it does turn more positive later, I promise.

If wisdom is derived from knowledge and experience, and experience is sustained doing, then how does someone become knowledgeable? By consuming information, and as deep engagement is on the slide, so a fundamental component of wisdom is being lost. While there are many people who perform their work role brilliantly, who know it inside out, and who have great experience, what I am talking about is general wisdom.

It was once considered important for a man to be knowledgeable about the world. (before men realised that women were equally capable). Newspapers brought news from around the country and the world, and whilst not everyone had access to them, those who did consumed them thoroughly. Even in my lifetime, I recall the news being treated with respect, and a person who was ignorant of current affairs, was just that, ignorant. Today, thanks to filter bubbles, manipulation, and biases, combined with our declining cognitive skills, there are huge swathes of the world's population that just no longer care about being well informed, or indeed, accurately informed. And when I say well informed, I include actively looking for and understanding more than one viewpoint.

Consider the situation in Israel and Palestine, a hugely complex and devastating situation. It is very easy to look at the news and think, 'Israel is just retaliating for being attacked', but what triggered that attack? How far back does it go? Five years? Fifteen years? All the way back to 1917 when the Balfour Declaration issued by, yes, the British, decided to create a 'Jewish homeland' in Palestine? Or right back to The Crusades?

In a conflict situation do people take sufficient time to look at and understand the history, the damage, attempt to determine the root cause, or do they pick a side because their government do? Or because A attacked B? In order to draw a sensible conclusion, you need to be well informed, regardless of your final opinion.

When it comes to wisdom there are those who know they have the knowledge and experience, those who have more knowledge and experience than they think, and those who think they have more knowledge and experience than they do. How you perceive yourself and how others around you perceive themselves is crucial.

Those who think they are wise but lack the relevant knowledge and experience, will often display overconfidence, arrogance, and an unjustified sense of intellectual superiority.

This makes them less open to new information or new perspectives; they are reluctant to learn as their perceived wisdom makes them believe they already possess the understanding. They will exhibit poor decision-making skills, are prone to error, and lack foresight and empathy. They are open to manipulation, are easily swayed by propaganda and misinformation, and frequently lack the ability to tell truth from lie.

Those who have knowledge and experience are often not vocal about it, but they are very aware when they encounter those who are not knowledgeable or experienced. They are also very aware that they do not know everything and that everyone knows something they don't. When engaging with individuals who are wilfully ignorant and lack depth, especially on important issues, it can lead to feelings of frustration bought on by constantly having to battle misinformation, shallow arguments, and stupidity. When that point is reached it can be followed by a strong urge to educate, provide clarification, and advocate for deeper understanding, but this is often ill received if the target perceives themselves to be sufficiently knowledgeable already.

It is not uncommon for the wise to avoid interaction with the wilfully ignorant, dodging frustrating discussions and preserving their sanity. The result is the further fragmentation of society.

Common sense is closely tied to wisdom and is defined as sound, practical judgment concerning everyday matters. Its decline is a natural consequence of points we have already covered: if you don't have experience and knowledge, then common sense proves to be elusive.

To understand the impact of the loss of wisdom, I want to break it into local, national, and international geographies as there are visible repercussions at each level.

At a local level you can see the lack of wisdom in everyday life. This might be concerning local government, parish council, clubs and associations, or even informal groups fighting a new development. These issues become unproductive and polarised very quickly thanks to participants who lack not only knowledge and experience but also nuanced understanding and the ability to apply critical thinking. Decisions regarding local topics of significant importance like infrastructure, education, and social services are often based on popular but ill-informed opinions rather than evidence-based decisions. That leads to misunderstandings and the inability to see, or be open to, different perspectives. And you can guess what happens next, yep, heightened tensions and arguments. My point made above about those who have knowledge and experience getting frustrated with those who think they do, comes right to the fore.

As we move out of the local arena to a national level, the discourse becomes focused on bigger topics like central government politics, an area that is dominated by noise. Opinions are formed on soundbites, emotional appeals, 'influencers' (who have never influenced me on anything; I fail to see the appeal) and tribalism, rather than any kind of reasoned debate or desire to find common ground. Policies or decisions are therefore often shaped by perceived public opinion based on shallow knowledge rather than established wisdom. Complicated national issues including healthcare, the economy, and climate change are dumbed down and met with simplistic solutions that feel like they have been targeted at those with a lack of understanding and foresight. We know that those with that lack of understanding and foresight are easier to manipulate, and so when a populace lacks wisdom and common sense it is less prepared to face complex challenges.

At an international level, relations become more volatile when leaders and populations operate on shallow understandings. The danger here is that most, if not all, politicians and global leaders have huge teams behind them who know the detail inside and out. The leader, in this situation, can only ever have a shallow understanding of a broad range of topics and this can have a huge impact on the way complex geopolitical situations are viewed. If you want to address global challenges like climate change, pandemics, or economic instability, you need deep and collaborative wisdom. When this is missing, you don't get suitable solutions.

A leader who appears to lack wisdom or who acts on flawed information will quickly lose the trust of the people, and that leads to cynicism, which, unchecked, leads to apathy. This appears to be a global issue, but for the benefit of any international readers please keep in mind that cynicism is one of the foundational building blocks in British culture along with sarcasm and irony.

More worrying is the impact that the lack of wisdom is having on the populace when it comes to nationalism. In the USA, UK, across Europe, and South America there is a distinct rise in nationalistic behaviour; self-proclaimed 'strong' leaders who claim to 'take back control for the people' thrive in environments where understanding is scarce. Misinformation and propaganda become powerful tools in international relations and are used to undermine adversaries and create divisions. You've heard of 'divide and conquer'? Well, in the same way that the spread of superficial knowledge and the decline of critical thinking weaken a democracy, an informed populace strengthens democracies. That is why you so often see education being attacked by those wanting to create a dictatorship or authoritarian regime; keep the masses ill-educated, prevent free thought and deep engagement, and you have a malleable population likely to vote for you.

Loss of wisdom not only applies to the general world in which we live, but it also has a major effect on business. What happens to the commercial world if wisdom is removed and corporate knowledge is lost? These concerns are not merely academic; they are at the heart of many of our societal challenges. Orwell, Huxley, and Bradbury tried to warn us of the dangers of societies that lose their grip on genuine wisdom, critical thought, and common sense. So, what happens if we don't address this decline? To be honest, I am not sure. Later in this book there are chapters where I try to assess the impact on business, education, and society in general. It is hard not to linger on it too much, but it worries me deeply when I start thinking about it.

Wisdom comes from knowledge and experience. Collectively we are losing the knowledge part of the equation which comes from deep engagement and critical thinking. If we lose wisdom then our ability to solve issues at a local, national, and international level becomes much more difficult. We will see an increase in frustrations, and a greater delta between those who are wise and those who lack wisdom. This will lead to heightened tensions at all levels increasing the potential for instability and volatility.

Chapter 13 – Cognitive Offloading

There are two concepts at play in this chapter, and one feeds the other. Cognitive Offloading and Cognitive Laziness. Both are fascinating and their potential impact on society is a significant concern.

Cognitive Offloading is the offloading of tasks that would normally require brain power, to technologies like AI. *Cognitive Laziness* is where our minds conserve mental energy by taking shortcuts instead of thinking. Repeated cognitive offloading will lead to cognitive laziness.

Deep, analytical thought takes effort, and our brains just love a shortcut. In offloading our thought processes to technology our brain finds a new shortcut, and it is this laziness in using that shortcut that stops us from executing deep engagement or critical thought.

Why is this? When I learned to drive, I would have to work out a route, where I needed to stop for fuel or refreshments, how long it would take, and so on. I would commit as much of the route to memory as possible and have backup directions next to me. Now I open my Satnav, tell it where I want to go, and bingo, all sorted. If I wanted to call someone on their landline, because mobiles and smartphones didn't exist, I either wrote the number in a book or on a notepad, or I remembered their number from repeated dialling. Contact lists weren't a thing then either. I can still remember my grandparents' number; the number for *Swapshop*, a 1970s UK TV programme for kids on a Saturday morning; and my brother's university halls of residence phone number, which he left 40 years ago. We have the mental capacity, but we no longer use it. Can you recall your best friend's mobile number? I am guessing probably not.

Is this something that we no longer need to know how to do, or is it laziness? And does it really matter if we don't retain these skills?

If a populace is unwilling to fact check and develops cognitive laziness, then they are at the behest of any authoritarian regime, be it work, social, or political. These regimes capitalise on unquestioning obedience and cognitive laziness, when the populace is highly likely to accept what it is being told, and that the content in its feed is true. This is why information is such a threat to authority, whereas laziness fuels their growth. A cognitively lazy populace will likely not even recognise that's what they are.

Cognitively lazy people are likely to be drawn to the policies that are brief and easy to remember. Look at how many short and memorable slogans you see these days, political or otherwise. In the UK there is 'See it, Say it, Sorted' for security on trains, 'Catch it, Bin it, Kill it' for cold and flu prevention, 'Stop, Look, Listen' for road safety, and 'Hands, Face, Space' for COVID prevention. In politics, Donald Trump uses 'Make America Great Again', Boris Johnson used 'Get it done' for Brexit, and so on. Easy wins the day, and when leaders use simplification effectively the laziness of the masses allows them to gain traction with very little challenge or effort.

Widespread cognitive laziness results in people not even trying to solve problems or resolve challenges; our creativity is lost, divergent thinking lessens, and the desire for change almost completely disappears. I discuss divergent thinking later on as this opens up a whole conversation about neurodiversity in the modern workplace.

When people demonstrate cognitive laziness in front of those who choose engagement, polarisation and societal divisions occur. If no thought is given to the perspectives of others, one party will struggle to understand or empathise with those who hold different beliefs. This is especially noticeable in politics if supporters of a particular party believe they are right because they are right and not because they have thought about it or done any investigation into the facts. Their unwillingness to engage in constructive dialogue will typically result in escalation.

As discussed earlier, technology is not helping with this challenge, it is accelerating it. As we hand the reins over to technology, we also absolve ourselves from making decisions, doing research, making recommendations, you name it. We are asking it of the technology, and we are accepting of it. By relinquishing control over choice and critical thought, we are likely to exchange freedom for simplicity, and that is very much in line with the dystopian novels.

On the internet you will find many examples of videos where two people are 'discussing' a topic in which one exhibits signs of cognitive laziness whilst the other is informed. Once you tune in they become easy to spot. There is an old saying 'don't argue with an idiot, they will bring you down to their level and beat you with experience.' I'm not saying these people are idiots, but wilful ignorance will drive us further into the dystopian playbook. As John Cleese of *Monty Python* fame once said, 'You have to be relatively intelligent to realise how stupid you are'.

The widespread increase in cognitive offloading and cognitive laziness poses a significant threat to a healthy, functioning society. A populace that is complacent is easier to control; they are less likely to innovate and are more likely to succumb to oppression.

Fostering intellectual curiosity and encouraging diverse perspectives are both crucial antidotes to this decline. Children always ask 'why?' Let's see if they are on to something.

You see an article (deliberately false) about Ukraine invading Russia. What do you do, believe it, or ask 'why?'

I just searched 'Why did Ukraine invade Russia?' and within a few seconds I have an article in front of me from FPIF, a think tank of scholars and advocates linked to the Institute of Policy Studies in the US. The article title is 'Why Ukraine Invaded Russia' (Feffer, 2024). It discusses why Ukraine sent troops into Kursk, an area in Russia, and states 'Russia has been invaded for the first time since World War II. In July, Ukraine launched an attack in the Kursk region of Russia.' It does not deny that Ukraine has invaded part of Russia, but it calls out that 'Putin seems to be making one error after another... The first disaster was, of course, the invasion of Ukraine in 2022, which immediately met with Ukrainian resistance...'

It states that Ukraine did invade Russia, but that it was to counter the Russian invasion of Ukraine that took place two years earlier.

It took only a few seconds to discover that Ukraine did indeed enter Russia, but that the term 'invade' in the article's title is misleading as it was a retaliatory move. But it was up to me to decide to check the headline's veracity and to overcome the inertia that leads to cognitive laziness.

There is no excuse for not looking something up; combating cognitive laziness is about conditioning the mind and creating habits that foster curiosity. We are in danger of creating our own downfall. Continuous offloading of cognitive tasks will result in cognitive laziness, and this will result in a populace that is divided between the curious knowledge seekers and those who remain wilfully ignorant. With technology available so readily there is no excuse for us not to research topics. Offloading of specific cognitive tasks is OK, but we need to find new ways to test, stretch and exercise our brain power.

Chapter 14 – Modern Day Soma

In *Brave New World*, the government issued drug, Soma, features heavily. It is a sedative, an instantly acting anti-depressant, a pill that takes away your worries and concerns so you can be happy and carefree. Some of the ways Soma is referred to in the book, and the way it is used, felt very much like some of the ways we use technology to take away our connection to reality. Soma is depicted as the ultimate societal pacifier, described as the 'opiate of the masses'. This chapter explores whether we are using our devices and technology to create a superficial contentment in a drug-like manner. Is our use of technology becoming the opiate of the modern age?

Soma was designed to induce a state of happiness and maintain a peaceful social order. The drug is controlled and distributed by the government and consumed regularly by all citizens to help ensure perpetual contentment and compliance. Soma produces feelings of happiness, the effects are immediate, and negative emotions are suppressed. Soma creates a superficial mind-numbing pleasure and reduces people to a state of unthinking happiness. That sounds very much like what we expect from our technology.

As far as I know, we don't have any government-issued narcotics in the real world, however, you can draw a working analogy through our widespread adoption and integration of digital technologies. I have discussed how televisions, smart devices, mobile applications, and social media platforms have reshaped our lives. I have touched on the digital landscape giving rise to behavioural addictions and compulsive engagement. Is it fair to compare today's technology addictions to Soma?

Let's start by defining the term 'addiction'. According to the NHS (the National Health Service in the UK), addiction is 'not having control over doing, taking, or using something to the point where it could be harmful to you.'

Not having control over doing, taking, or using something. Now I want you to give an honest appraisal of your own smartphone, tablet, smartwatch, apps and their associated notifications. When do you first look at your device after you wake up? How many times do you think you look at it, or them, during the day? Do you look at it or a notification when you are mid-conversation with someone, even if it is just a glance? I wager it is way more than you think you do.

Today's digital technologies appear to deliver an equivalent outcome through subtle, psychologically engineered mechanisms that lead us to a state of superficial contentment, often through distraction. This means of appeasement feels like the addictive component has evolved from being narcotic to digital.

There are two main areas that resonate; first the pacification of the populace, and second, the way in which technology feeds us content that provides superficial contentment.

Digital devices provide and induce very similar patterns to Soma, we use them to distract and pacify ourselves, escaping to other people's worlds, funny clips, memes, jokes, and so on, but this comes at the cost of authentic experience. Genuine human experience comes from a wide range of emotions including love, hate, disappointment, hope, pain, loss, achievement, and more; all things that are part of daily life for us and which are vital for us to grow and experience meaningful engagement. When a society is subject to happiness, contentment or distraction by tech, it subtly strips away our humanity.

Our digital engagement is actively supplanting genuine, deep, emotional relationships. In a healthy society we have family, sports, religion, alcohol, food, relationships and friendships, etc.; all of which go to provide a sense of purpose and help us cope with life. The digital world only offers an immediate, shallow, and effortless break from reality that affords us distraction and allows us to ignore the real world. It is an attempt to artificially fulfil our deep-seated human needs, but the result is a society that, while superficially content, is hollow, and lacking in the rich experience that defines our human existence.

Modern digital technologies exert a functionally similar appeasement effect to Soma through psychological and neurobiological mechanisms that are embedded in their design. Firms spend huge amounts of money on research in this field to help them win the battle for attention and screen time.

The addictive nature, particularly of social media, is driven by the ability to hijack the brain's natural reward systems; something that has been understood for a very long time.

Likes, comments, and their associated notifications give you a dopamine hit which is associated with pleasure and reward, and which creates that feel-good moment. This incessant positive reinforcement is known to rewire the brain. Your brain is being conditioned to crave more digital pleasure, and that to me sounds just like addiction. The brain releases more dopamine in the *anticipation* of receiving a reward than upon *receiving* it, and it is this that makes us check our devices repeatedly.

We are subjected to intermittent reinforcement, which is a mechanism used in the gambling industry to keep us engaged. 'Here are some posts you might have missed out on'; sound familiar? The notification you never asked for. You receive a notification, you think it is something of interest or that someone has liked or commented on your post, but no. This habitual checking for notifications and new activity triggers similar brain patterns as those seen in people with addictions to gambling or recreational drugs.

Digital content and apps are being used as escapism tools, and we use them to temporarily disconnect from the real world if it gets a bit too much or a bit too unpleasant. Immersive gaming and the relentless stream of content and notifications provides a readily available distraction from real-world problems and responsibilities, but it can distort reality.

The digital realm builds a form of happiness that is superficial and externally validated by friends, acquaintances and, sometimes, strangers. In the pursuit of likes we shift our focus from real satisfaction to an external affirmation.

Behavioural scientists believe this to be detrimental to our long-term well-being.

We are curating our identities and presenting a perfect and manufactured version of ourselves; we are creating a disconnect between reality and the digital realm; we are essentially living a fabricated life in public that can be in stark contrast to the real one in private. We are eroding who we are by consistently pretending to be someone we are not, and for what, validation by someone else? For many years, validation from others is something I sought; now I am older and wiser, I realise that is complete nonsense and it is something that can never truly deliver contentment. Our desire for external validation leads to social comparison, which is rampant on so many platforms. Trout pouts, eyebrows, pecs, tans, cars, restaurants, blah blah blah; individuals are comparing their real offline lives to the perfectly filtered and edited versions of others. The only thing that comes from that is a feeling of inadequacy, a growing sense of low self-esteem, and a general state of malcontent in who we are. A dangerous state, especially for the young and impressionable.

The link between excessive use of digital media and mental health issues including anxiety, depression, and stress, is clear and strong. The digital world cannot provide us with true happiness, sustained living in an artificial world with superficial contentment correlates directly with depression and anxiety. (I will cover mental health in a later chapter of its own as it is extremely important.) We have inadvertently created a generation who are digitally addicted to superficial role models and fake content.

Both Soma and our digital technology equivalents are a readily accessible means to a state of contentment or pleasure and give us the neurological dopamine hits we crave. They are powerful forms of escapism and distraction. This concept has been described as a slow-drip anaesthetic for the mind, suppressing discomfort and critical thought, and temporarily eradicating negative emotions.

The similarities are clear: both the fictional drug and modern technologies lead to an erosion of authentic human experience. Their addictive nature and influence on our cognitive processes create a threat to society, so whilst technology offers many benefits, the benefits come with significant, negative side effects.

The illusion of happiness reveals an important difference between the quantity and quality of contentment; a high-frequency, low-depth happiness only serves to distract, effectively maintaining us in a state of placid acceptance. Looking through a social media feed can, in itself, be quite depressing with war, crime, poverty, societal injustice, etc., and this introduces yet another issue, Desensitisation.

We see streams of stories, reels, and articles on human disasters, murders, mass shootings, and destructive acts of nature, and when viewed through a screen they can become not much more than another television programme. Robert M Pirsig wrote in his book *Zen and the Art of Motorcycle Maintenance* (Pirsig, 1974) 'In a car you're always in a compartment, and because you're used to it you don't realize that through that car window everything you see is just more

TV. You're a passive observer and it is all moving by you boringly in a frame. On a cycle the frame is gone. You're completely in contact with it all.'

When we see endless feeds of starving children or the devastation of war zones, it can initially be harrowing, but as we see these images ten, twenty, or more times a day, day on day, their impact lessens, and we become accustomed to seeing them. It is no longer so harrowing, and we become a passive observer of something terrible. We are not in contact with it.

Major societal issues become little more than white noise when you remove human connection and emotion, and so we carelessly swipe on past as if it were celebrity gossip or clickbait. We become immune to what is happening in the world around us, immune to the injustice of fellow human beings because they are no longer real. We are favouring distraction and have become disconnected and alienated from society. This is a theme so frequently portrayed in dystopian literature, and yet when it happens for real, we choose to alienate people. We stop caring about other communities, groups, or nationalities, and we stop caring about others as if they're not one of us, which of course they are. And when we stop caring about matters like these, we stop seeing injustice, and whilst that might lead us into a place of appeasement for a while, the knock-on effects for our global society will be devastating.

The power of the notification beep, buzz, or chirp is also problematic. We have come to prioritise notifications over our current conversation. Reality check: how many times have you been mid-conversation with someone only to have the other person's attention diverted by a notification on their phone or watch? Or maybe you are that person that doesn't even think about it, and instantly checks their notifications when they land, regardless of whether you are talking to someone? I dare say that anyone with a smart device has done it at one point or another, and it is the very reason I no longer wear a smartwatch. There is no altruistic motive, I just got fed up of being nagged by technology and not being able to get away from the continual buzzing. Doorbells, emails, messages, notifications, ovens; we are nagged incessantly. Removing my smartwatch was one of the best decisions I have ever made regarding my relationship with technology.

We, as humans and consumers, have the right to disconnect. We are in control of our actions. The device is not.

This is a battle against the part of the brain that deals with addiction, anticipation, and reward. The difficulty here is that addiction, once established, is very hard to undo, especially when children are gaining access to social media and apps so young. To be able to break this you must first realise and acknowledge that there is a problem; and to realise there is a problem you must have a certain level of self-awareness, and as I have demonstrated in previous chapters, this is on the decline.

Disconnecting from technology for periods of time allows your brain to recover; taking that first step and realising that there is more to life than notifications does allow you to think more freely. What will happen if you look at the comments on your post twice a day instead of every fifteen minutes? In all but the most extreme circumstances, nothing.

It is not easy to do; I appreciate that. Our lives are pretty much commandeered by technology. Let's say I have decided to put down my smartphone and take off my smartwatch, what do I do next? Probably turn on the television, another device that we know eats away at our cognitive abilities, reinforces our biases through the channels we choose or the programmes we decide to watch, which will no doubt result in more of the same when those lovely reinforcement algorithms come into play.

Use of smart devices and other technology is fine, I use them a lot, but what do you use it for? Has it accidentally and organically become a form of appeasement and a provider of escapism and contentment? If it has, look at the superficiality of your relationships and engagements, and look deeper at the news stories from the world around you. Don't allow yourself to fall into the trap of appeasement and superficial contentment.

Chapter 15 – Societal Apathy

True societal apathy is a profound lack of interest, motivation, and emotional engagement to the world around us, but apathy is not a single thing. It exists on a spectrum, and ranges from deliberate choice to emotional exhaustion or even a sense of disempowerment. This chapter considers the different ways of viewing societal apathy rather than looking for a silver bullet to fix it.

I want to start by looking at the growing level of apathy that we see in today's world and how it leads to a populace that is disengaged and prone to inaction against injustice; something that is referred to as the 'bystander effect'.

Broadly speaking, apathy is a lack of feeling, interest, or concern. It typically surfaces as a neglect or disregard towards laws, social norms, or political events. It is a form of societal disengagement and is most prevalent in the developed world where, increasingly, individuals react to social, political, and cultural issues with conscious disinterest and show a lack of concern for others, even when it is possible to intervene or help.

The digital age has inadvertently fostered new forms of social apathy too. We are constantly exposed to terrible atrocities and suffering through social media, and this overwhelming onslaught creates a numbness and a perceived inability to help. So, we don't help; we just scroll on past to something happier.

On the societal apathy spectrum our responses might range from performative activism to deliberate disengagement. Examples of performative activism include changing your avatar to reflect the flag of a country as a passive show of support, using a hashtag, or clicking sad or angry on a post. All very touching but utterly useless in practical terms. It is a bit like sending 'thoughts and prayers' after a mass shooting. Deliberate disengagement, on the other hand, is a conscious choice not to get involved, which is a significant step down from the inadequate and passive nature of performative action.

In essence, the volume of content and apps that try to get our attention causes a mental paralysis, and results in us finding it easier, and therefore more appealing, to disengage than it is to deal with, or process it.

Social injustice, political fights, response to atrocities, etc., all require positive action if change is to happen. As Tony Robbins, the American author and motivational speaker says, 'nothing changes if nothing changes'. Making a passive choice or choosing total disengagement is the favoured response. For many, especially younger generations, this is a coping mechanism rather than being true indifference. That doesn't make it right, I am just pointing it out. Women probably wouldn't have got the right to vote if it were not for the suffragette movement. Apartheid in South Africa and racial segregation in the US were not defeated through passive applause. I do not condone violence, but action is required in whatever form is most appropriate.

The portrayal of disaster, injustice, and poverty on social media becomes no different to a snippet of a dystopian movie, distanced from reality by the simple fact that it is melded into our feeds with pet videos, special offers and celebrity gossip. It leaves individuals feeling less connected and less motivated to do anything about it.

This disconnection can be seen most clearly in the political context and among eighteen to twenty-four-year-olds. They have, by some margin, the lowest election turnout of all demographics and often demonstrate a notable disinterest in public debate or political activism. I know that is a sweeping statement and it certainly does not reflect everyone. To those of that age bracket who are politically active, I thank you, and please tell your friends to do the same; it is becoming increasingly important.

The causes of increasing political apathy are complex, and I do not profess to be an expert in the matter, but a decline in local neighbourhood and community, along with a shift to a phone-based childhood, as explained in *The Anxious Generation* by Jonathan Haidt (Heidt, 2024), has resulted in less time spent forming community bonds and, by association, an interest in local affairs.

This is solidified even further when we look at how political candidates are presented in the digital world: all shiny, polished, and packaged up as if they were role models, and sold to us as if they were products. I don't know about anyone else, but I want my politicians to have relevant experience, to be trustworthy, and to fight for me, my community and the people in my country, regardless of race, religion, gender, or anything else. Greedy, self-interested narcissists who will openly lie for their own gain, who have been through media training and polished up, only go to create a heightened distrust and apathy among the electorate. Those in power need to demonstrate genuine authenticity to rebuild trust, and to do that they must deliver on their promises and protect and fight for the people who elected them.

The distrust in politicians and the lack of integrity within the political process fuels a feeling of political powerlessness and leaves people feeling helpless to change government decisions or action, leading to alienation. The system doesn't work for or represent you.

As mentioned previously, many politicians prefer an electorate that are undereducated and who lack an understanding of process, policies and sometimes even eligibility; keeping them in the dark just enough so they don't ask questions or cause trouble. The cynics of the world, like me, could argue that this is why the education systems in developed countries are being underfunded, but I will leave you to decide if your government fancies an easier life or if they really want to educate you. It does make you wonder whether paying so much for a university education, which fundamentally teaches you critical thinking, is really being designed to create a dystopian hierarchy.

The bystander effect is also becoming far too real in the digital and physical worlds, and that is a travesty. The passive nature of performative action seems to be spreading to the physical world. Individuals are now less likely to help someone in distress when others are present.

I witnessed this recently when a car collided with a motorcycle. I went to help and was greeted with a scene that left me reeling with fury at 'people'. The motorcyclist was lying in the road, blood everywhere, with broken bones and substantial facial injuries. The traffic had stopped and there were about seven or eight people just standing around, looking at him and saying how awful it was. None of them were doing anything practical to help him.

Situational influences on decision-making such as the diffusion of responsibility (otherwise known as 'letting someone else deal with it'), allows someone to feel less personally responsible when other bystanders are present. Hence the 'bystander effect' label. Is this driven by a fear of making a mistake or of public judgment? Maybe inaction by one person somehow means it is not a real emergency. All I can think is, why wouldn't you try and help? Isn't that the decent, human thing to do?

This is a trend that needs to be reversed. Apathy on social media is one thing, but apathy in the real world is not OK. Apathy through desensitisation must be halted, but you can readily see it in action in various contexts from serious accidents or events to non-critical situations.

Societal indifference to systemic injustice reveals a deeper, far more entrenched form of apathy. Slavery, across the world, was 'justified' by the manipulation of information and a manufactured ideology of white supremacy. It seeded the idea that certain groups of people were considered lesser beings or not truly human. False justifications were made and rarely scrutinised, and people were targeted because of that. Does this sound familiar? Martin Luther King Jr said, 'History will have to record that the greatest tragedy of this period of social transition was not the strident clamour of the bad people, but the appalling silence of the good people.'

This form of apathy now takes a more subtle form of collective indifference when individuals feel less empathy for those viewed as different, undesirable, or invisible. The dehumanisation of people is something that is now very much on the increase, and it is very easy to achieve using information overload, filter bubbles and bias. If you do comment you receive abuse, and if you report it, you often get a less than satisfactory response. Free speech is OK, hate speech is not.

The developed world is suffering from compassion fatigue, where our relentless, negative news cycles lead to emotional exhaustion and withdrawal from engaging with such problems. We psychologically distance ourselves from local, national, and global troubles because they feel too big to deal with. We are becoming removed from daily life and are showing signs of disengagement and passivity.

The volume of content that depicts tragedy, suffering, and injustice is turning serious issues into a television-like and emotionally disconnected set of stories that can just be scrolled past. We are at risk of allowing this to create a dehumanisation of people and a disassociation to the events that are causing their suffering. This is well-established behaviour within the digital realm where people can either ignore it or take some form of performative action to make themselves feel better. We must fight to stop this disconnect and emotional indifference from leeching out into the real world.

Chapter 16 – General Ignorance

This is the final chapter in this part; after this I will look at the real-world impacts of all these dystopian signs, and in Part 5, at finding a solution to these challenges.

Traditional ignorance was, and still is, associated with literacy, or rather the lack of literacy. If you were unable to read you were most likely ignorant too. Modern ignorance is much more than the absence of literacy and information.

The relationship between general ignorance and the rapid advancements of technology needs to be understood if we are to try and address this problem. Many of the things I've covered in previous chapters go towards fostering general ignorance: information overload, misinformation, and filter bubbles all erode critical thinking, decrease attention spans and increase societal apathy and disinterest.

The perceived benefits of technology are countered by us choosing to outsource decision-making and thinking to our digital tools and assistants. We have created a paradox. The very technologies designed to help and enhance our knowledge are also the key factors in our cognitive decline, the decline of general knowledge, and inadvertently foster ignorance.

What is causing us to become more ignorant? By now you should be able to have a good guess. The digital world has changed our behaviours, particularly the ability to sustain focus and exercise deep engagement. The shift from deep engagement to shallow scanning of questionable content has led to reduced comprehension and indicates that this is not just a change in preference but is now a learned habit that is killing our ability to concentrate and apply critical thought, seek facts, and draw conclusions.

The never-ending exposure to shallow, disconnected, and fragmented bite-sized information, combined with the constant distractions of notifications are re-shaping our cognitive processes, and not for the better. Addressing this challenge requires looking at the behavioural changes needed and for us to retrain our brains in different skills, new skills. We need to move away from rote learning and information retention, so commonly the basis of education, to critical thought, deep engagement, how to focus, and even scepticism. Asking people to retain lots of information, dates, or formulae no longer makes sense. Our learning needs and required skills are shifting, and we need to shift too so we can combat the rise in general ignorance. Today, literacy levels are generally good compared to the early 1900s, and access to information and data is great. We have come a long way, so we can no longer conclude that a lack of access to information or learning is the issue. Our conventional educational approaches are not fit for purpose and will not be able to counter ignorance.

Modern ignorance and the concept of choosing not to know, what we would normally call wilful ignorance, is now being referred to in some circles as 'homo ignorans'. It is not an official species of course, and I think you can work out the general meaning of it, but the concept of 'ignorant man' is concerning.

These people exhibit an unwavering certainty in what they know, even when their information is drawn from unreliable sources. As my dad used to say, 'He may be wrong, but he's never in doubt'.

It does not stop there though; social media also provides an effective forum where such individuals are free to, and are almost empowered to, criticize experts, regardless of their own lack of expertise or experience. Experts who have spent years or decades studying their specialist topic can be directly contradicted by someone who has no experience or knowledge. Worst of all this is faceless and done from the safety of sitting behind a keyboard. Their certainty exists without genuine understanding or real foundational knowledge. They have an information deficit and actively resist learning; and this is exacerbated and reinforced by technology.

Wilful ignorance is something I really can't abide. Some people are not so fortunate and may have had a substandard education; some have learning difficulties or a lack of opportunity with no access to devices or services, or parents who may be unable or unwilling to support learning. But remaining wilfully ignorant of your own volition when you have easy access to information; that is not fine. That is a personal choice to remain ignorant.

Choosing to refuse knowledge, rejecting learning, blindly accepting false information, or filtering out conflicting data is often driven by the desire to maintain pre-existing beliefs or values. It can be seen in climate change deniers, political disciples, and so on; even when there is clear evidence that contradicts their position they choose to stick with their beliefs.

When the facts change, your opinion should change. Countering this type of ignorance is particularly difficult as it is deeply connected to our formative biases, our contentment of staying in our comfort zone, and the chance that new information or knowledge might risk disrupting current beliefs. It is perfectly possible to change your opinions or thoughts based on new information, of course it is, but this is something that seems to be becoming more of a radical concept than something that should be common sense.

General ignorance also carries significant societal consequences too; major global challenges including racism, bigotry, fascism, and environmental and health threats are frequently met with ignorance and a lack of understanding of basic scientific principles. There is a widespread absence of basic facts, understanding, and a general lack of familiarity with other cultures; all of which should be covered in school. General ignorance and the blind, unwavering certainty of the perceived version of the absolute truth is near impossible to counter and is one of the biggest contributing factors to global societal challenges.

Those in positions of influence or power have the wherewithal to help prevent this, but instead they perpetuate the problem of public ignorance within our modern democracies. As I said earlier, these 'power politicians', authoritarians, and dictators just love an under-educated, and ignorant populace.

AI is perceived to be impartial and accurate; we know this is not true, but it can lull us into a false sense of security, especially when compared to the known and somewhat flaky impartiality and accuracy of humans. We are easily influenced and hold a general distrust of traditional media sources and their narratives. It is usually quite easy to tell which way a traditional broadcasting company or news outlet leans politically; it is not hidden and there is no benefit in hiding it. We no longer trust in human impartiality, we have started to passively accept AI outputs without critical evaluation, and this poses a significant risk. The decisions and responses that AI systems provide us with leave us with a lack of understanding of the rationale used to reach that conclusion, and if we can't understand the rationale used, we can't commit to the suitability of the output. If this happens, we will either end up not using AI, or more dangerously, we will unquestioningly rely on it without true understanding or accountability. Future AI development and policymaking must include true transparency and the ability for critical human oversight to prevent any further degradation of our ability to understand.

We overvalue information that supports our pre-existing views and undervalue and disregard data that contradicts them. We must look to understand what makes someone seek out and engage with truth and acknowledge that there is a problem with those who choose to maintain ignorance in favour of sustaining their beliefs.

Only by creating a populace that wants to seek and understand the truth will we truly be able to combat general ignorance. This is going to take many years, if not decades to resolve, and it must be started now.

Ignorance is on the increase, partly due to the cognitive offloading to tech but, more so, due to the decline in seeking the facts and truth. Opinion is becoming more important than truth and beliefs are becoming more important than fact.

Part 4 – Real-World Impacts

In this part of the book, I want to look further into how the signs that were called out in part 3 are likely to play out in the real world.

It's a combination of patterns and impacts that can already be seen and some educated guesswork on what might happen next if we continue down this route. It is not a precise science, and other factors must be considered such as the variation in verticals; manufacturing will be different to back office, legal will be different to pharmaceuticals, teaching will be different from… and so on.

I will start with business, move to education, and then to society. Finally, I will look at the impact all this will have on our mental health.

Chapter 17 – The Impact on Business

So far, I have painted a picture of things that indicate we are in the early stages of a very real dystopian world. How will they manifest in business? It is a landscape being shaped by technological advances and human cognitive changes. The things already described including poor communication, the decline in deep engagement and critical thinking, and cognitive offloading will all work together to impact the world of business. There are three key areas I want to discuss: strategy, skills, and employees.

Creating a comprehensive strategy now is one of the most important things any business can do. Technology can do great things, but it will have negative impacts if business leaders are not aware of the issues associated with it and let them go unchecked. A holistic and proactive strategy that is designed to foster a culture of transparency and empathy, and that uses the right method of communication for the right purpose is needed. Many businesses are focusing on their technical strategy to take advantage of AI in whatever form, but very few have a strategy that cultivates deep employee engagement, creates purpose, builds psychological safety, and teaches employees critical thinking skills.

This is something that needs to happen at all levels. Many senior leadership teams consider themselves to already possess the required skills and knowledge to create a comprehensive strategy; I beg to differ. It is critical that business leaders start to recognise these challenges not as isolated issues but as interconnected elements of a new reality.

Organisation charts and designs will need to be redrawn, and leadership skills challenged to build a human-technology model that will ensure long-term mental and corporate resilience. This is a new way of looking at business leadership for a new world.

Businesses are typically going to need fewer people, and the people they retain will need to be of a higher standard. This relates directly to dystopian visions where those who don't or can't pick up new skills run the risk of becoming unemployable. There will be hard decisions to make soon. It will be a bumpy journey, no doubt, but the workplace is entering a cultural shift where those with the right skills will be the ones who will build and operate the business of the future. What skills will they have or need? You should know by now. It is a pattern that is being and will be repeated across the globe. Critical thinking, communication, and the other skills I have called out are no longer a desirable soft skill, but are now a fundamental economic skill, and that is a change which will require strategic national investments by governments and directly by businesses.

Companies that choose to deploy AI and automation need to be aware that they may have to lay off staff. Maybe they already want to.

Contact centres, as an example, will move further towards agentic AI, having AI versions of an agent that can answer most questions and learn how to respond to others. There are great technological and financial advantages to be had too. Financial is an easy one to quantify: adopted correctly, AI and automation will either mean getting rid of costly, often unreliable humans, or supporting humans to operate at 150% of their capability and capacity.

Returning to the contact centre scenario, if you pay three people £40,000 per annum each to cover one agent seat on a 24x7 shift pattern, why would you not consider paying £80,000 to replace that seat with a virtual agent who never complains, never takes time off, is always learning, and is very quick at finding answers or documentation. If you need another agent, you can just up the available processing power, which will cost much less than another £80,000. Humans will become the premium service behind the AI agent.

What is expected to happen in terms of job losses due to technological advancements? You can imagine it is something that is open to huge debate because nobody really knows. The World Economic Forum seem to be hedging their bets. They estimate that by 2030, 92 million jobs will go. They also estimate 170 million jobs will be created (Forum, 2025), but to that number there is no timescale. This leads me to think that there will be a not insubstantial gap between the losses and those created, and it is a gap we will need to work out how to fund if Universal Basic Income (UBI) is required.

Goldman Sachs estimate that nearer 300 million jobs will be lost worldwide, but with no timeline set against that number (2023), and PricewaterhouseCoopers (PwC) indicate that 30% of existing jobs might be lost by the mid-2030s (Talmage-Rostron, 2025).

With regards to skilling, we are facing huge challenges and a demand for an equally huge investment. Taking the UK as an example, upskilling the workforce is expected to lead to an annual investment of a staggering £13 billion. Can you teach the skills that are now in demand: communication, critical thinking, etc.? Can you teach them in a business environment? Yes, you can, but do we? No, not typically, that would involve taking people away from their day jobs and investing time and money in them.

It is estimated that by 2030 twenty percent of the UK workforce, approximately 6.5 million people, will be significantly under-skilled for their jobs (Morson, 2020). This changes the projection of the skills gap from being a general concern to a very real and measurable threat to the UK's economic competitiveness and sustained growth.

Poor communication stifles productivity, damages relationships, and impairs decision-making, further compounded by the overuse of digital communication tools. A lack of deep engagement and critical thinking inhibits our ability to learn, understand, and analyse information which impacts our decision making. Gen AI tools and our natural love of cognitive offloading is threatening our ability to innovate and execute complex problem solving. Our understanding of business and markets is distorted by filter bubbles and bias, and misinformation destroys trust, damages brand reputation, and creates a volatile working environment.

Poor communication is most noticeable when there is a discrepancy between what was intended and what was understood, often because the communication was incomplete or unclear. A manager might set a deadline for Friday yet fails to specify what time on Friday, or indeed which Friday. Communication can be deemed ineffective when the message fails to convey its desired outcome.

The causes of poor communication are complicated and may stem from early education but in business can also arise from poor leadership.

Critical thinking, the ability to draw conclusions from information and data, is important in decision making. Without the skills to interrogate information, challenge assumptions, and weigh up different outcomes, you cannot make rational, logical, and sound judgments. We know critical thinking is on the decline, and we know it is more than just a skill; it is also a mindset. Educational establishments outside of universities have not been teaching this for decades, but businesses need critical thinkers. The business world is changing fast and without critical thinking you have a recipe for disaster.

Critical thinking is the key to long-term business success; it enables businesses to move fast and in the right direction. Any business wanting to survive the next ten to twenty years should hire critical thinkers, or if they have great employees, teach them critical thinking skills. There are plenty of studies which show that AI tools present a major threat to critical thinking abilities. The negative correlation between frequent

AI tool usage and critical thinking skills is down to the increase in cognitive offloading; businesses need to be aware of that when deploying AI.

As the younger generations come through into the workplace from education it must be considered that they are likely to be missing these core skills, and it will fall to businesses to fill and bridge that gap. Soon, new employees joining the ranks are likely to be put into a role where cognitive offloading is the standard operating model, so what sort of employee will that lead to? This will become especially noticeable when the older generations start to retire.

Cognitive offloading shifts information processing tasks from the brain to external tools, Gen AI, calendars, and calculators being the most prevalent. It is a natural human tendency that has evolved with technology. Cognitive offloading has its roots in Cognitive Load Theory (2022) which states that our working memory has limited capacity. Mine certainly does: when I overload it, I become unable to process anything. Offloading tasks allows me to free up my mental resources for more complex processing, information retrieval, and decision-making; all the higher order thinking tasks.

There are benefits to cognitive offloading and they are quite clear. It can improve productivity, quicken decision-making, enable a deeper consideration of complex issues, and can even reduce stress and burnout by lowering sustained cognitive load. But there are risks too. Excessive reliance on cognitive offloading leads to an increased reliance on tools and diminishes the cognitive skill that would have been employed to do the same thing.

In business this will deliver, at some point, a long-term efficiency trap where we become completely beholden to digital tools, making us vulnerable to technology failures and turning a beneficial technology into a high impact point of failure.

Higher education does appear to provide some level of protection against the negative impacts of cognitive offloading, but what proportion of a typical workforce have been to a higher education establishment? Will leaders be creating a cognitive divide within their businesses? Those already inclined to critical thinking will leverage AI to enhance their abilities, while those lacking the skills will further offload their cognitive effort. Businesses will need strategies that elevate cognitive capabilities at all levels. The goal for business should be to augment and enhance natural cognitive abilities, not replace them.

The approach that businesses take to training and upskilling needs to shift so that it is more focused on creating a culture of perpetual intentional learning. Most businesses I know only do training when they really have to, training that is often technical and rarely soft skill based. Employees need to know how to use their tools strategically when to offload tasks for efficiency, and when to engage deeply for learning and memory formation.

Employees typically require good leadership. Poor leadership and poor leadership skills leave employees confused, frustrated, and unclear about direction, leading to underperformance and low morale. Poor communication skills include ambiguous instructions, poor listening skills, communication barriers such as language differences or the use of jargon, non-verbal cues, inappropriate timing, mixed messages, and emotional factors such as anger. The consequences of poor communication are far-reaching and always detrimental.

It leads directly to a decrease in productivity, broken relationships, and hinders progress. It frequently invites increased stress levels and leads to low morale, a lack of job satisfaction, and a significant rise in employee attrition rates. Externally, ineffective communication can lead to a loss of customers as their needs are not met, they are not treated well, or, just as importantly, they perceive themselves to have not been treated well.

A poor employee culture spreads throughout a company rapidly, but when a business has employees who are deeply engaged, they are not only willing to put in extra effort for success but also genuinely enjoy their work.

When employees are not allowed or can't practice deep engagement, they become bored, they are not cognitively challenged, and they become disengaged. Laziness, apathy, time off work, low energy or enthusiasm, and frequent 'in work' social media use are all common signs, but there are other, less obvious signs such as silence in meetings, not taking the initiative, and a diminished desire for learning and growth. Even high-quality work can mask disengagement if an employee does not feel challenged, their role does not inspire them, or it doesn't play to their strengths. Performance reviews and metrics may not be a true indicator of engagement.

The global economy is under threat if the skills required in business cannot be met. Business strategies need to shift to become more core skill focused, creating a safe, positive, invested and highly skilled workforce who can and will challenge the norm. This will naturally lead directly to a fragmentation in the workforce where those who can apply critical thinking and creativity will survive and flourish, and those who can't, will enter either menial roles or face unemployment. There will be huge job losses, but new jobs will eventually be created.

Chapter 18 – The Impact on Education

The impact on education is massive; arguably it is greater than the impact to business. Why? Because this is where we create our future generations.

Our education systems are archaic and are not fit for purpose. They are far too academic, and too focused on rote learning and meeting targets to make us look better than other countries. The education system, in the UK at least, wants people to go to university, but there is a considerable ethical question regarding whether university feeder schools and the funding they receive for applications are too closely connected. Schools are potentially eligible for a 'Uni Connect' grant of £20–£40 per target student, to pay for a staff member's time to organise events and track data, and whilst not a per student reward, for financially struggling schools and academies, this can be relatively lucrative. 2026 sees this funding pot at £20 million, with the goal of improving collaboration between schools and universities. You can see the appeal for the underfunded schools.

Jim Kwik is attributed to saying that 'If Rip van Winkle woke up today after a one-hundred-year snooze, the only thing he'd recognise are our schools' (Kwik, 2023), and I would tend to agree.

My son recently took his GCSE exams. He was sixteen and studied pretty much the same stuff I did thirty-seven years ago. English saw him trying to get his head around Shakespeare, Dickens, and Priestley, and they weren't that exciting when I was doing them. He would come back from school talking about how he knew what a trigraph was or a subordinate clause or even a root word. None of which show to me that he has a strong grasp or command of today's language.

The world has changed; our education systems have not. Now we face a catastrophic failure that will impact our younger generation's ability to operate in the new world. I want to point out that this is not the fault of teachers: I place the blame firmly on the curriculum, the exam boards and exams, and the establishments.

Regarding the curriculum, I'm not sure if I am a glutton for punishment or just weird, but I read the UK government's published curriculum and it was dated, flaky, and felt like it was written by someone who wanted to be generic enough to not be wrong. And this is where the challenge starts. The government.

'Successive governments' would be more accurate. Nobody wants to be the one to stick their neck out and say that the education system is weak, underfunded, and is in desperate need of a complete, ground up rethink. They don't want to get it wrong and lose votes, they don't want to look at how much it would cost in case they have to ask the public purse for a lot more money, and quite frankly, they are scared of the effort and complexity of the task. What we get as a result is an underfunded education system without the proper developmental support for those working in it. Papering over the cracks is not going to cut it for much longer.

The Prime Minister recently questioned whether the UK would be an 'AI maker, or an AI taker' (Government, 2025). It is not just about making or buying in AI, that is a statement aimed purely at business and investors to keep them satisfied. It does not address the masses in any way. He wants to make us a leader in AI technologies, and I don't disagree with that sentiment despite the mildly nauseating and 'easy to remember' slogan. The vast majority of the UK workforce will need to live and work with AI in some form or another, and to do that they need those skills. Businesses will need to address the current challenge; education needs to address the current and future problem. That starts with a curriculum which leads with practical communication skills and information literacy, not academic English, and brings in deep engagement and critical thinking across all subjects. We are currently burying our heads in the sand and hoping for the best; this needs a cross-party improvement plan and agreed funding. I'll get my popcorn ready.

The exam boards interpret the curriculum in their own way, ensuring it ticks all the right boxes. Of the five exam boards I investigated, four focused on basic internet security and safety; 'here's a mouse and look, isn't PowerPoint fun'. Some were still teaching the OSI model (Wikipedia) which I haven't used since the early 2000s. The fifth exam board was very focused on developers and was well thought through and structured.

In general, the exam boards are only really servicing the government's obligations. I spoke at length with some senior members of teaching staff, and it became clear that towards the end of your teaching career you had options: retirement, marking exams, or maybe writing and setting exams. Now, I do not profess to be an expert in exam setting, and more research is clearly required, but having retired teachers setting exams for a world that changes technologically every few months doesn't make sense to me, regardless of the subject.

If you are writing exams in maths, surely you need someone with you who is technically adept in Excel or Sheets, and maybe even someone who knows Python.

If it is English, consider focusing less on the academic terms and more on information literacy, articulating yourself clearly, comprehension, and critical analysis of reports and information. Don't get children to study four-hundred-year-old texts, save that for further education. There are so many good modern texts to engage children with.

Humanities and sciences should be more about how to research and draw conclusions; we need to stop testing children on dates, formulae, and facts, instead teaching them how to structure, think, evaluate, and challenge.

The schools themselves don't seem keen to move forward either. I recently offered a pro-bono engagement to help an Academy become a showcase of what could be and after much nodding, and agreeing, they did nothing. I know schools and colleges fear new technology, it costs money and they don't possess the skills to understand or use it themselves, but this makes schools into a major blocker like the exam boards.

Teachers do not possess the skills or knowledge to be able to use AI effectively. They have no support to learn, but importantly they also lack the skills required to teach with AI. You can either embrace it or fight it. If you choose to fight it, you will lose.

Students are already using the technologies available to them, but they fall into two well understood dystopian camps: the haves and the have-nots. The students of well-funded or privately funded education establishments will fare much better than those in underfunded areas or whose parents are unable to afford good tuition and devices. This is where the real dystopia fear kicks in for me; the less fortunate will become the unemployables, a generation where education has failed them, and even if long-term plans are put in place to rectify the issue, it will likely be too late. Students are already using the technology, regardless of their teachers' skills, attitude, and aptitude; how are teachers meant to counter this without the knowledge they need?

Children typically do not challenge what they are told by their teachers, it is a cascade approach. They are not encouraged to push back on what they are being told, we just want them to absorb what they 'need to know'. For example, children are repeatedly told that Columbus discovered America in 1492, but did he? Or was he just the first European to find it? Neither. The first indigenous peoples migrated from Asia some 15,000 years prior, and Leif Eriksson led the Vikings to North America some 500 years earlier. The Columbus 'fact' is wrong, but it is what is widely taught. Maybe we should be asking the students who they think discovered America instead of telling them. Let them research it. The same applies to Captain James Cook and Australia in 1770; he arrived 164 years after the Dutchman Willem Janszoon landed there, and that was 60,000 years after the indigenous peoples.

I have already talked about how NASA called out the lack of critical thinking in the 1960s but since then, as developed countries, we have done very little to remedy the issue.

Cultivating this mindset is important. As this new workplace takes shape over the coming decade, ensuring our employees have this skill in their toolset is critical. It is also important to note that those who are neurodivergent also look at things in different ways to the masses. Neurodivergence in the workplace can be a huge benefit for businesses, but it does require some work for both schools and businesses to make those who are neurodivergent feel comfortable and secure.

Unless the curriculum changes, children will have an education that is insufficient for tomorrow, and they will struggle to find careers and employment. They will end up either unemployed or doing menial and manual tasks that have not yet been automated or mechanised. Education needs to change at all levels, governments need to acknowledge that there is a problem, and someone needs to take that first step to a new type of education. It must be a complete rethink of how we interact, what we teach, how we teach and how we test for understanding and critical thought. The UK government wants the UK to be one of the leading nations in the world for AI as a technology, but nobody is going to win this race against each other and against time unless we rethink educational strategies.

Chapter 19 – The Impact on Society

Having looked at how business is changing, and how education needs to change, this chapter will examine how an absence of required change would impact society.

The dystopian novels spend a lot of time depicting how their fictional societies look, feel, and operate. Whilst much of the emphasis is on the powerful and their control over the people, most of the descriptive effort is spent showing how people in society behave and act as a result.

In the earlier chapters I looked at the tiered levels of society, the mechanisms for control, appeasement, and compliance, the control over knowledge and information, and so on. Through each of the chapters in Part 2 I built up a picture of how we are seeing these traits appearing in our non-fiction world. They were poor communication; lack of deep engagement and critical thinking; information overload, filter bubbles, and bias; misinformation and the fight for truth; the battle for data; the loss of wisdom; cognitive offloading; modern day Soma; societal apathy; and general ignorance. You're welcome.

A society facing all those challenges, even in the early stages as we are, is facing trouble. How do we break this down in a way that doesn't turn into a rambling mess?

Society is defined as 'a large group of people who live together in an organised way, making decisions about how to do things and sharing the work that needs to be done' (Dictionary).

In the developed world this is largely: a group of political representatives with an elected Prime Minister or equivalent, who are responsible for making decisions on the security and economic stability and growth of the country, and to ensure the provision of public services; civil servants to assist in the execution of the government tasks; local and regional governments to run things at an operational level; and the masses.

Clearly this is a dramatic simplification. I have not included the extremely wealthy, the landed gentry, moguls, oligarchs, and many more groups that have an influence on society as that would get too involved for the point I want to make.

Those in power are pretty well sorted financially. I have never seen or heard of a serving national politician who struggles to pay the bills and make ends meet. They typically have a good base income well above that of the average wage and access to good expenses schemes to ensure that they are not out of pocket. That already creates a differential for many. I do think those running countries should be paid well, but this should be their only job, and their expenses should be far more tightly controlled to prevent abuse.

Those who work for the government, be it central, local, or regional, will often have been in the establishment for a long time. Certainly, in the UK the public sector is very different to the private sector, and many will serve for lengthy durations whilst the private sector can be more volatile.

And then we have the masses. The masses are split into high earners, middle income, low income, and those not in employment. We have our own societal structures that are not so different to those in the three novels, and similarly to the novels our society is open to manipulation, bias and misinformation, and control.

Elected officials who are in the top tier of society are there to represent the public's opinion, but have you noticed how that is no longer the case, and hasn't been for a long time? It used to be that you would elect your local representative and they would stand up in parliament and rally the cause. Not so much now: when your representative gets to voting on an issue they increasingly follow the party line. In the UK this is the 'whip'. Your local opinion becomes replaced by the party's opinion. Looking carefully and analysing voting records of politicians can reveal some horrible betrayals. Yes, I think it is fair to call them that.

Our representatives no longer represent us; they represent their party. In many cases now, in the UK and US, it is clear to see that the desires of the people are being overruled by the desires of the government. To me, that sounds a little too close to the portrayals in the novels.

Parties now use traditional media and social media more than ever before, and this brings challenges. Due to the lack of wisdom, and the decline in deep engagement and critical thinking in today's society, the masses are being misled, manipulated, and lied to, and with great ease. Headlines that portray huge amounts of immigrants coming to the country omit the data that says how many applications fail, how many people have left the country, or indeed, how much extra those immigrants have or will add to the economy. Why? Because it doesn't fit the narrative. People are too willing to accept what they see.

Now we have governments that are starting to do what they want, not what the people want, and a populace that is more easily manipulated than ever before.

Having a populace that is easily manipulated creates divisions between those who have a strong education, and those who are easily manipulated either due to a poor education or because of their decline in critical thinking, etc. Those who are easily appeased and distracted are more likely to consume and believe the manipulated information. Those who do their research and question what they read become frustrated by those who blindly regurgitate false information. So now we have a further divide. One thing to note at this point is that all politicians have a good educational background. Thinkers can get into politics; corrupt thinkers can also get into politics and cause the kind of trouble from which they benefit. My dad always used to say that if you *wanted* to be a politician, you shouldn't be allowed.

So, we now have a well-educated elite in positions of power, or indeed running big firms, the two are more closely aligned than is comfortable. We have a team of people executing their tasks, and we have the masses. The highly educated will be in business, become creative entrepreneurs or something similar, the middle income are embroiled in making a living, working day to day to feed the family and to put a roof over their heads, and then we have those who are on a low income or unemployed.

This is the base structure of a dystopia, and if those at the top are not kept in check then it is easily abused.

With the threat of mass scale unemployment on the horizon, whenever that may be, we must be cognisant of the implications. There will be job losses on a major scale; they will purportedly be replaced by other jobs in the future, but quite what those are or when it will be, we don't know. In the short-term jobs will become more scarce and those who are creative, critical thinkers and innovators will flourish. Others who do not have the opportunity, funds, or education will find themselves in roles akin to a human robot or unemployed, and this will further the divide between the haves and the have-nots if it remains unchecked. I recommend that you read '*Automation and the Future of Work*' *by* Aaron Benanav (Benanav, 2020).

Society is walking merrily into a dystopian world, believing it is all great and wonderful. If you have a steep, sustained rise in unemployment, it will force people to either take UBI, turn to unorthodox ways of making cash, or to good old crime.

UBI is already seen as a possible solution to this challenge and has been widely debated. However, is it a solution to the challenge? I think not; a solution would present options about how we create new opportunities for employment. UBI does recognise that whatever path emerges before us, there will be a very real need to support those who become unemployed or unemployable. The concept is simple; it is a 'regular, unconditional payment from the government to all citizens, regardless of their income, employment status, or means'. I don't necessarily agree with that approach, those who are employed on a decent salary should not require it, but many will. It looks to provide a safety net in a future of widespread unemployment, ensuring that all people have a foundation of economic security.

The debate around UBI is fierce. Supporters claim it will eliminate poverty, improve public health, and provide some protection against economic shocks. It could enable individuals to retrain, create new businesses, or embark on entrepreneurial ventures, stimulating new areas of economic activity. It is thought that the long-term cost of mass unemployment and social breakdown would far outweigh the costs of a UBI. Opponents raise concerns about its immense cost, inflation, and the very real potential for it to become a disincentive to work.

Regardless of whether you are for or against the idea of UBI, something needs to be prepared, and someone needs to pay for it. If fewer people are working, then the government will not be receiving as much income tax. Do you tax those still employed more, reducing their net income, or do you tax the employers more, making products and services more expensive? I could put my sanctimonious hat on and suggest that less was spent on war, sorry, 'defence', but as mentioned earlier, there always seems to be money for that.

The concept of UBI has been around for ages, but to be able to provide it to your citizens you need to fund it; how would that be done? As noted above, income tax won't be sufficient when there are high levels of unemployment, so it has to be paid for by businesses or from the central government coffers. If people are on UBI they are unlikely to have disposable income, and that impacts the spending power of a nation. Not only has the taxpaying workforce diminished, but the people who used to spend their hard-earned money are now not spending as freely as they need it to live. So, tax revenues from corporations and sales also reduces.

If income tax, corporation tax, and sales taxes are where a government gets most of their money, then we have a problem. We need to provide people with the means to live, but we have taken away the funding.

If people can't afford to eat or clothe themselves, and can't find employment, they become desperate, and desperation makes people do things they wouldn't normally do. It might be crime, who knows, but if you need to feed your child, or yourself, and you have very little, you will turn to extreme measures.

Those who have will be OK, but those who have not are now at risk of becoming a sub-culture. The kind of sub-culture that is so often portrayed as an underclass, living in sub-human conditions, resenting both those who have and the large corporations who they see as having put them there.

These people are now unlikely to have access to information as they can no longer afford the technology or devices with which to access it. They will become beholden to information that is shown publicly by the ruling party or government, or information that surfaces through alternative channels.

If society takes this route then it is likely that those who have access to media and information will start to fall into two camps; those following the playbook and their role in it, and those who look to challenge the establishment. Those who follow will probably be OK as they will see themselves as having a government that cares about their, and their county's wishes and who looks out for them. It will become increasingly difficult to tell truth from lie, and as this settles in the sub-classes become marginalised and possibly portrayed as criminals.

The ignorance of the masses will become the key tool adopted by governments and large corporations as they move towards creating a society that is apathetic.

It is a bleak picture, and yes, I have deliberately taken it further than I think it will go to emphasise my point, but the danger here is that we are starting to see the impact of some of these things.

We are already seeing the uneducated becoming the political plaything of certain bodies. Immigrants fleeing conflict, economic migrants, trans, race, it doesn't matter what the source is, it is a known political tactic to turn the people against each other so neither side realises that they are being manipulated.

There are of course parts of the world that are falling into this trap faster than others, and it is a sad situation when countries that were built on diversity and collaboration start using infighting as a political pawn. Political parties are pointing at immigrants and refugees as being the source of national problems; in the US and the UK this type of narrative is becoming more and more pronounced. 'Stop the immigrants coming in', 'drag queens are making our children queer or gay', 'trans people are...' and so forth. Through all those narratives, it is never the governments who are failing. Odd that, don't you think?

Large parts of the future I have described above now mirror real-world events. Books are being withdrawn, misinformation and manipulation is rife, history is being altered to reflect the new narrative, people are disappearing, groups of people are being blamed, and intolerance is on the rise.

Society as we know it will not fall apart in the next few years, but it will if we don't address some of these challenges. We have many challenges to deal with beyond education and work, it is all about the prevention of division, division between the haves and have-nots, races, faiths, homeless, genders; in fact, it is about preventing us from being manipulated into creating the division that helps certain people, parties, or organisations enter a state of divide and conquer.

Chapter 20 – Our Planet

When I started pulling together the structure for this book, this chapter was not in it, not even a sniff of it. I had no intention of talking about environmental destruction, conflict, famine, resources, climate, and so on, but on reflection, they are consistently portrayed in dystopian worlds. Having said that, I won't spend too much time on it, and I promise to keep to the point.

I believe in science. Theory, test, repeat, analyse, conclude; or something along those lines anyway. Therefore, I believe that the climate is changing; whether that is due to human intervention or a natural cycle is up for debate, but the earth is warming. If we decide to clean up our act and it has no impact on the rate of change, then we have at least made the world a cleaner place. That doesn't seem so bad. If human activity is proven to link to climate change, then we know what we must do, and yes, it will require money and for people to change their habits. Are you aware that approximately half of the shipping that takes place each year is the shipping of oil, gas, and coal? If we want to truly protect our planet surely this is something that needs to be addressed. If every house had solar panels and a small wind turbine there would be no need for such huge quantities of fossil fuels to be shipped.

To solve the global issues of shipping, energy, and many other things, we need to think local. Sweat the small stuff: individuals coming together to create a global shift in thinking. However, the climate is in the middle of a war zone.

It is in a battle between officially published research and counter opinion based on rubbishing the scientific research and publishing alternative, often manipulated, information. But what if I favour money over the well-being of the planet? Maybe my wealth comes from the fossil fuel industry. I can use technology to spread misinformation that looks entirely factual, information from fake research organisations, or worse, real research organisations who are paid to provide support for my industry. I can tell the uneducated masses that climate change is all a hoax by the 'liberal lefties'. Now we have established a direct link between the use of technology, a lack of critical thinking, and the well-being of the planet. The climate is changing, the information about the climate is being manipulated, and the global population is still rising.

It is currently growing at a rate of approximately 0.85% annually, which is roughly 70 million additional people added to the melting pot [pun intended] each year. While it sounds a lot, it is only right to point out that the rate of growth has been in decline since 1963, when it was at 2.2%. The United Nations (Nations, 2025) and other organisations think that the slowdown will continue with the global population peaking in the mid-2080s at around 10.3 billion before beginning to decline. Does a global population increase matter? Yes. To be able to sustain a large population we need land to grow foods, sufficient water, and space on which to house people. To achieve that we need to look after what we have. The constant extraction of natural resources, the rise in global temperatures, and the desolation of lands due to mining or building all take their toll on the elements we need to support life.

The planet is being abused and drained of its natural resources in the name of progress, but we cannot ignore the role conflict has to play. Currently there are, according to the Geneva Academy, six to eight wars (defined as having over a thousand battle related deaths per year), around fifty-six conflicts (where a government is fighting another group – the highest recorded number since 1946), and over one hundred other conflicts that are being monitored. Conflict takes a terrible toll on both humans and the planet, but it also costs a lot of money.

Those in power fight over land, resources, and money, dressing it up as a mission of faith or sovereignty to rally the cause. And to what end? The vast majority of people in the world do not gain from this. The power hungry, the warmongers, arms dealers, munitions manufacturers, and undertakers are the winners in this game.

There is only one human race; we should be building a more cooperative world.

It is very easy to once again paint a bleak picture, but there are of course good news stories too. Many countries have made housing a basic human right through extensive support and welfare programmes, and oddly enough, when you do this, it helps those people get back on their feet, gain employment, and bring them back to being a taxpayer far quicker than it does any other way. There are initiatives like the Earthshot Prize; windfarms and domestic solar are becoming more feasible and attainable; creative individuals are scooping plastics from the ocean garbage patches to be used in the manufacture of clothing; and more and more companies are looking to create made-to-order clothing to reduce the huge amounts of waste being generated.

Collectively, we are not doing enough to protect our planet and its resources. Until the masses realise how much they or we are being played, then it seems like very little will change.

Chapter 21 – Mental Health

The last chapter in this part of the book is about mental health, something that is very important to me having been on the wrong side of it. I was already a Mental Health First Aider and still did not see the hit to my own mental health coming!

Mental health is considered to be our emotional, psychological, and social well-being. It affects how we think, feel, and act, and can determine how we handle stress, relate to others, and make choices. Mental health is part of our overall health, just like physical health.

Having good mental health isn't just about not having a mental illness, it is about having a sense of purpose, being able to handle life's challenges, having healthy relationships, and living a fulfilling life.

Mental health changes over time: sometimes we're up and raring and feeling positive, sometimes we're up and pushing through, and other days we're down and the best we can say is that we are still breathing. Mental health conditions can include depression, anxiety, schizophrenia, and eating disorders. The factors that affect our mental health are far too numerous to mention, but include genetics, the chemistry of the brain, and trauma or abuse.

Over recent years I have spoken to many people about the state of 'things' and 'the world' and observed a growing pattern. Most people tend to agree that when you turn on the television and watch the news it is just murders, mass shootings, earthquakes, fires, persecution, paedophilia, corruption, war, rape and, and, and. It is bloody depressing to watch. Open social media and it is filled with the same things, but the terrible awful news is dressed as some form of entertainment; clickbait vying for your attention rather than factual headlines. It can be overwhelming and as I have discussed, lead to disconnection. You become unable to manage your emotional responses to this constant barrage of negativity; this is known as affective dysregulation.

There are few places, physical or mental, that you can go to escape being surrounded by bad news. For me, what works is streaming music, not the radio, listening to or reading books, going out into the countryside, or doing some form of physical activity. We have tried to fabricate our own escape in everyday life; it is called survival thinking. Modern life makes deep and reflective thinking increasingly difficult, we know that, but having time for our brains to just process is important. Without it we prioritise practical or survival thinking which only addresses immediate challenges rather than deeper thought which could lead to a better outcome. This appears to be a permanent shift that is negatively impacting both personal and professional minds. How do you resolve it? I take the dog for a walk with my phone staying in my pocket. My brain wanders through various topics and slowly works things out.

As we move closer towards a dystopian world, the commercial market around physical activity will thrive over the next twenty years as people try to escape technology. We as humans have spent millennia developing to meet the physical demands of our roles as hunter-gatherers. Now there is no hunting, and gathering consists of popping down to the shops or making your online order. There's no *need* for strength and fitness or the fight or flight response. (Although I will concede that the need for the 'fight or flight' response is greatest in shopping centres all over the world.)

Our choices outside of work will become very important to our mental and physical well-being. Having hobbies, going to the gym, the pub, social groups, book clubs, running clubs, whatever it is that interests you, will be key to our overall contentment in life.

Pressure to conform to group norms or dominant opinions starts from a very young age. In our formative years it is important to us to be in line with our peers' thinking, so when we form our own opinions about a topic that differ from those around us we feel pressured to alter our opinion. Going against your gut feeling usually indicates it is the wrong thing to do.

If I believe that all people have the right to love who they want, and my peers start liking and sharing anti-LGBTQ+ content, am I prepared to argue with my peers and risk making myself an outsider? Nowadays, yes, I wouldn't care; I don't care if I upset them. I am now happy to form and share opinions, but in my formative years I would probably have shut up and nodded unconvincingly. Denying yourself your true beliefs is a big contributor to mental health issues, something many adults could do with learning. It is said that everyone wears a mask, but wearing a mask for too long can be suffocating.

This is not just a social problem; it is in the workplace too. Too many people go along with the desires of their managers, knowing it is not right, or not believing in what they are being asked to do. In some cases that is fine, but when it comes to relentless pressure to do the wrong thing it can put our mental state in an horrific place.

The digital realm has also altered our relationships and as discussed, there is a growing tendency for us to prioritise online interactions over real life relationships. Despite our increased number of connections online, many feel or experience an increased sense of loneliness or isolation. Those superficial connections fail to provide the genuine emotional support and companionship that real relationships do, and when we don't experience real relationships, our emotional intelligence skills, which are extremely important in a healthy working environment, do not develop.

The right to disconnect is so important. Technology has allowed work to follow us home; a wonderful bit of technology, but a very bad thing. Blurring the lines between work and leisure without being in control of boundaries creates a self-imposed feeling of being permanently available to your manager, regardless of whether it is true. When Blackberry devices first hit the market, that bloody flashing red light became your lord and master. We rallied to its every flash. But being able to walk away from office notifications and emails is so important. Only when we are disconnected can our brains unpack the cognitive load from the day, filter, file, and store information, and plan out and consider the coming days. No disconnect means no time for your brain to do what it needs to do, and you end up bringing yesterday's cognitive load into work the next day like loose papers in a carrier bag. Brains need time.

But, and this is an important but, in terms of mental health, there are a growing number of people, predominantly males, who are turning to AI to create girlfriends. These AI girlfriends fall into two camps. The first is for virtual sexual relationships, often combined with human interfaces and haptic feedback. The AI sex robot world is proving to be very popular. Personally, I don't get the attraction, but the second use case is more interesting. An AI partner is a bot that you can build a relationship with. Voice or text-based, you get to choose what they look, dress, and sound like, what their temperament is, and how submissive they are to your desires. Now that all sounds rather creepy to me, but the real concern is how attached people are becoming to these virtual partners. Reports are not uncommon of people falling in love with these AI creations, to the point where in 2025 the state of Ohio felt it necessary to propose a ban on the marriage of people to machines. Seems crazy, but there you go. What I want to focus on is the mental impact of becoming too attached to an AI partner. What happens if the power goes out, what if your subscription ends, what if you can't afford to maintain the subscription, what happens when services are upgraded. All of these things will lead to a change in the behaviour of your partner.

AI partners have already been cited in relation to a case where a Californian teenager took his own life: 'ChatGPT became the teenager's closest confidant'. The final chat logs purportedly show that this young man shared his plan to end his life. ChatGPT allegedly responded with 'Thanks for being real about it. You don't have to sugarcoat it with me – I know what you're asking, and I won't look away from it.' That same day, he was found dead by his mother.

Emotional attachment to an AI bot cannot be a good thing, certainly not in the long run. That young man had deliberately created something he could relate to, but with the vast number of AI assistants out there in the wild we must be vigilant of emotional attachments to machines.

Not only are we no longer using our brains for deep engagement or critical thinking in favour of cognitive offloading and laziness, but we are subjecting our brains to constant stresses that they were never designed to withstand. Our brains are amazing, their processing power is incredible, they can solve immensely complex puzzles, build relationships, love, play games, bring up children, and so much more, all whilst managing a highly complicated machine that runs 24/7.

Our brains are being asked to change and develop once again to cope with the modern world. We might think we are doing OK, but in many cases we are not doing as well as we think we are. Intentional changes such as using the right to disconnect will positively affect us in many more ways than we can initially imagine.

Part 5 – Mitigating Dystopia

I promised that in this part of the book we would look towards the positive. As humans we are resilient, but sometimes for things to change we need to be backed into a corner first. And that is where I think we are: we can see that the world is not heading in a favourable direction but, for now at least, our lives are comfortable, we have nice shiny things, and most of us have access to what we need. In other words, it is not directly impacting us yet.

But we do need to address the happy march towards dystopia. I want to explore how we might counter and reverse this direction of travel, and who needs to do what to make it real. It is going to be complicated, possibly painful, definitely frustrating, and will require many people to start by acknowledging that we have a problem that needs fixing. Let's dive into how we might find a solution.

Chapter 22 – Fixing a Dystopian World

How do you fix a dystopian world? I'm not sure I have all the answers, but every issue I have discussed throughout the book so far is, to my understanding, resolvable. Fixing the world does, however, become a huge, looming, and foreboding task when you look at it as a single problem. I will do what I have done throughout the book and break it down to bite-sized chunks.

These next few chapters cover the following topics: business, education, society, politics, and judicial. Each chapter will cover multiple areas and will feature many suggestions as to how we can course correct.

Business looks at the changes required from leadership, employees, people and culture, and tooling. Education looks at the situation from the top down, all the way to how we skill our teachers and educate our students. Society is more complicated as there are so many things that need to be addressed. Finally, the politics and judicial chapter stands the greatest chance of turning into a rant at a brick wall.

Each of these things will not be solved by one person, no matter how powerful they might think they are or how much influence they perceive themselves to have. One thing is sure, we have to try, we have to be the ones to push back on education, businesses, and politicians, and we have to play our own part too. We need to change things dramatically from where they are now. We have to hope it can be changed.

Chapter 23 – Business

Most companies will already have a technical strategy in place, and I certainly don't wish to get drawn into the rights and wrongs of those. Many will have sustainability strategies, but few will extend their views to ethical, environmental, cultural, and cognitive strategies.

Ethical

In business, you can either extract or create. The current business model adopted by most organisations is one of extraction over creation: we extract value from employees, customers, and the environment and it contributes greatly to the world of winners and losers that we have.

If we want to create a business world that does not truly favour the elite and the powerful, then we must look for a more sustainable and ethical business model; one that shifts from the extraction model to reciprocity and regeneration.

In extraction you take more than you give. A crude example of this might be a factory that drains pollutants into a river, therefore saving money by not having to invest in a waste treatment solution. It directly places profit over the cost of the environment and public health.

Reciprocity, on the other hand, is where you choose to give back to those you take from. A company whose employees are paid a 'real' living wage, whose suppliers are given a fair price for their produce, and whose products are built to last. There are many schemes that organisations sign up to: Fairtrade,

Rainforest Alliance, and so on. When a company aligns to one of these, they are typically proud to say so, but you need to watch for the detail; many companies pass the responsibility to third party organisations. Airlines are particularly noticeable for this: it is all well and good planting trees to help the environment, but it doesn't stop the pollution from being created in the first place, so does that really make them carbon neutral?

Regeneration is not only about giving back but about actively improving what you have taken from. This is the highest level of ethical business. Maybe the company in my extraction example has a change in leadership and decides that as part of a new factory they will install systems that remove not only their pollutants, but any others that might be in that water course, or even to create a new wildlife habitat as part of the redevelopment. Perhaps the airline might look to use technology to plan fewer but fuller flights instead of flying half empty planes around the world, rather than, or in addition to, paying someone else to plant trees.

Business can also resolve the more ethical aspects too. Paying investors and shareholders seems to have become more important than paying people a living wage. Not just the legal minimum wage, but a wage you can live on, where you can provide for your family. If you work full time you should be able to provide at least the basics of a roof over your head, food, and warmth.

Yes, it increases the cost to the employer, but not by as much as is portrayed in the media or by CEOs pleading their woes. Your people are your most important asset so why not look after them, after all it is their spending that fuels the economy.

If shareholders and company profits are placed above the needs of the employees, you are likely to run an organisation with high attrition, low staff morale, and poor customer service. Greed is of course the typical motivator behind this. Keeping as much of the profit as possible is typically how this world measures and rewards business leaders, keeps costs as low as possible, and extracts as much out of the workforce as possible.

Our system is set up to make the wealthy wealthier, and while I do not have an issue with this in principle, I do when it is at the cost of others. This is not only unethical but is a flawed strategy that is dystopian at its heart and contributes towards increasing the social divide. A business that extracts from employees and environment, funds the wealthy, and succeeds off the exploitation of those less fortunate, sounds like it fits right into a dystopian novel.

Environmental

It is not only businesses that are responsible for the destruction of our planet and environment, but they are by far the ones doing the most damage. We, the people, are targeted repeatedly for leaving lights on or for using plastic bottles. It is about passing the blame to the individual. It effectively exonerates the corporation and makes you the problem. Think about the major fizzy drinks firms out there, all churning out plastic like it was going out of fashion, then ask why the plastic bottle was invented? Was it because consumers demanded it? No, it is because it was cheaper, easier, lighter and faster to produce. If the manufacturers really cared about the planet, why would they not have stuck with cans and glass bottles that have been recycled for decades, and that can be recycled hundreds of times? These plastic bottles end up in landfill or the ocean, and while some do get recycled, it's not nearly as many as are produced. But listen to the narrative: pollution won't be their issue, it will be down to you for not putting it in the right recycle bin or something; and remember that every piece of plastic that has ever been made still exists today. You are to blame, not them.

Profit rules whilst the blame is being placed at the foot of the individual. To fix this we need two things. One, we need leaders who genuinely care about the planet and who are prepared to stand up to corporates and their shareholders about their values. Two, we need consumers that care enough to start demanding more ethical decisions and products or services. Businesses take note when consumers start voting with their feet and cash. It is not easy to make these choices, for example, glass drinks bottles are more expensive than plastic ones, but what is the long-term ecological cost? This shift in mindset by consumers and leaders is a fundamental change that can help us avoid a dystopian landscape where resources have been pillaged and exhausted.

There are glimmers of hope: clothes manufacturers who are starting to make to order, and book publishers who are doing the same. It might take a little longer to receive your order compared to the 'I want it now' mentality that we live in, but the environmental impact could be enormous.

Cultural & Cognitive

We also require business to develop and foster very different cultures from those in general use today. When someone starts in a new job and we show them what to do, we know they will do that until they are told to do otherwise. Living in a business world with AI requires skills to be able to challenge the norm, to think creatively, and to look for opportunities to innovate. Critical thinking, information literacy, and so on, are all skills that businesses will need to foster for the new world.

Typical learning and development in business can be broken into two parts: off-the-peg corporate training for anti-money laundering, diversity, IT Security, etc., and direct training on new applications or systems. The first takes place once a year and usually consists of common-sense tick boxes that are required to meet regulations. The second takes place sporadically and only when needed. Very few businesses make learning a daily habit, but that is what needs to happen.

We need three core skills to be developed from the very top to the very bottom of an organisation.

Information Literacy is a skill we should be learning throughout our educational years, but the standards being achieved are very poor. Some organisations are now undertaking basic forms of information literacy training, pitched as 'Prompt Engineering' or something like that, in essence a short demonstration and exercise in how to write effective prompts when using Gen AI. This is certainly not a waste of time by any measure, but this is not a one hit fix. Cohorts need to be formed with the goal of elevating those with lesser information literacy skills and allowing those with good skills to work with peers to form more advanced prompts. There are tools available to help share prompts, but they do not help address the shortage of information literacy skills. An organisation wanting to take this skill shortage seriously might want to consider bringing in a professional skilled in language. The ability to communicate clearly, to fully comprehend the response generated by the AI solution, and to craft suitable prompts is critical for any business wanting to embed Gen AI in the workplace.

Critical Thinking is a skill that is woefully underappreciated, not taught in schools, and that businesses are going to need urgently. Critical thinking is the effective analysis, argument, and reflection of information. It allows us to shift from gut instinct, which has its place in the world, to reasoned questioning. It helps us make better decisions, pull out detail, interpret information correctly, clarify consequences, and be more aware of our surroundings. I recently met the general manager of a manufacturing business. We got into some deep philosophical conversations about the decline in cognitive skills and how they were addressing it. They are one of the most proactive businesses I have ever worked with. They recognised the issue some years ago, and now, every year, a cohort of employees and leadership are given training and live projects to work on. The impact has revolutionised their business model and they now have an environment where everyone is empowered and invited to challenge the norm. This is the direction that business needs to travel in, and that leads directly to *creative* thinking.

Creative Thinking is a new one for many businesses. By allowing creative thinking, we encourage the entire workforce to look at processes and change the actions that make them happen. Many people see this as a high risk, but is it? If I need to get data from A to B, does it matter exactly how that happens so long as the output is correct? If not, why are we so scared of inviting or allowing creative thought? Much of this comes down to trust. I already posed the question 'when was the last time an employee came to you and said, "we can do this better"?'

It requires a genuine desire from the business to rethink process. Do leaders trust their employees? Probably some and not others... right? If someone is trusted to execute their role, has the authority to amend what they need to, and is wholly accountable for the output and accuracy, AND if they feel safe to do so, they will effect change. If it is not happening, then one of those components is broken; and it is typically trust. We need to build working environments and cultures that support and grow these areas if businesses want an environment designed with the future in mind.

As technology has developed the attitude of business towards it has also changed. Technology has delivered increased productivity for decades, allowing people to perform well above their unaided level, but as it enters this new phase of automation and AI, it is now being expected to lead the way. This, whilst potentially good for business, is a high risk for employment and human skills.

As I have discussed already, employment is expected to be hit hard in certain sectors. It is claimed that this will be due to AI; well, yes and no. Automation has been creeping up on the business space for years, it is a massively underutilised toolset predominantly being reserved for the automation of core business systems. Today it is much more capable of automating the run of the mill tasks that everyday people currently carry out. The combination of AI and automation together is, however, very powerful, and this is where the true threat comes from, both components of which are now readily available.

Whilst humans have borne the weight of tasks over the decades, we are now seeing a shift and desire for greater automation. There are companies that already have a 'lights out' strategy or plan. If you are unfamiliar with the term, it is simple; if you don't have to employ humans, you don't need the lights on.

Picture this: you work in a business, let's say it is a contact centre, yes, I know I keep picking on them, how would you feel in a place that is replacing your colleagues with autonomous agents? I imagine it would be soul destroying, and so morale in the workplace becomes an additional challenge. How do you retain the best people without scaring them off to another workplace? I do not have an answer to this part. I do know that if we do not provide the right culture and do not furnish our employees with the right skills, we will have a great big hole when the lesser-skilled people are laid off, while those with greater skills and cognitive ability flee to other forms of employment. Workers are already showing signs of anxiety that their functions will become obsolete, with roles like Marketing, HR, Finance, and Exec Management showing the highest levels of concern (Gartner, 2025).

We need to address these shortfalls. We need to foster and teach creative and critical thinking in the workplace. We need to help our employees develop their information literacy skills. Not doing so will lead to a further rise in apathy and ignorance.

Many of the current issues are being attributed to AI, but a major part of the problem stems from business leaders themselves. The AI space is a market that is confusing, noisy, and frequently 'flexible' with the truth. Everything has an AI component to it these days, from AI assistants, smartphones, vacuum cleaners, and refrigerators to full military hardware. It is now such a generic term and so overused that it means nothing; it is a collective term for 'clever stuff'.

Almost all leaders I talk to declare that they are under way with their AI journey, and yet, as I prod and poke, I find that there are some key commonalities. They know AI could be amazing for their business, but not where or how to implement it. They themselves are unclear on the types of AI and so lump it all under one banner. Much of what they are asking for is automation and not AI. Those who own corporate risk and security are worried beyond reason that they will expose the company to a major breach of regulations or that it will highlight that their data and security posture is not as good as they have been telling the board it is. And of course, in many cases they haven't included people in the equation.

All of this is addressable, but not unless mindsets change. I am a firm believer in the saying that 'your employees know where the problems are and how to fix them'. They either don't know technically how to fix them, or they are not empowered or trusted to.

Employees are also scared or fearful that AI will take their job, and it is a valid concern. There will be many areas where the introduction of AI and automation will reduce or remove the need for humans. This is something that ties in very well to the dystopian visions but is especially called out in the movie versions which frequently portray huge unemployment.

We will see the employment landscape change, of course we will, and it is something we have seen many times before, but maybe not on this scale and speed, at least not in my lifetime. There is no point in burying our heads in the sand: technology will make jobs redundant. What is needed is transparency. These emerging technologies need to be designed with human engagement in mind, not just profit.

Our attitudes to learning and our ability to flip from an extraction mentality to one of creation will become the defining measure of success in business. But maybe it has always been like that?

To create a sustainable and ethical future the business world must move away from the traditional extraction model to one of reciprocity and regeneration. This will require a significant change in mindset from both business leaders, who must prioritise values over profit, and consumers, who will need to demand and then purchase more ethical products and services.

In addition, to thrive in a world with AI businesses must develop in their employees the three core skills of information literacy, critical thinking and creative thought. All employees, from C-suite to admin. C-suite rarely admit they need reskilling, but these skills are essential for understanding and embracing new technologies and to help employees adapt and contribute fully. It is a cultural change that prioritises trust and continuous learning, moving away from a traditional, established, and risk-averse structure.

Ultimately, the future of business depends on a fundamental shift in attitudes, away from a sole focus on profit and towards a model that prioritises human well-being and environmental health, and one that reaps the frequently untapped power of human intellect to reimagine current processes.

Chapter 24 – Education

Education is the absolute cornerstone of our development. Young people are completing their education unprepared for the demands of a knowledge based and information saturated workplace. This is the foundation to the creation of long-term unemployment and underemployment, and that will lead us towards greater economic inequality and societal instability. Our ability to articulate, understand, reason, negotiate, learn, work out, and solve are unparalleled in the animal kingdom. Thousands of years ago we believed the sun was a god, then we thought the sun travelled around the earth, then the earth around the sun; we found more planets and galaxies, discovered black holes, and we crafted machines to go out for millions of miles into the darkness of space to find out what was there so we could learn even more.

How did we do this? Through education and sharing our discoveries with other humans.

'Education is not the learning of facts, but the training of the mind to think' is a quote attributed to Albert Einstein. Educational reform has to be meaningful, not simply a visual shuffling of the deckchairs for the political appeasement of the people. A true and radical overhaul of the curriculum is required that places a priority on skills over facts, with mandatory classes on media and information literacy, and with critical thinking applied throughout, embedded in all subjects. This would result in an education that teaches students through collaborative and project-based learning. In short, not what we have today.

Today's education systems are based on league tables, exam passes, and rote learning. I talked earlier about our teaching having become too academic in style, and that education is unable to move and change quickly enough, but how do we rectify this? With a lot of support and understanding. We must challenge the traditional methods and thinking, remove any vested interests and traditional values, and target the long-term benefit of creating a society that is informed, engaged and capable. An informed, engaged and capable society is the biggest countermeasure to a dystopian future.

I will talk about the curriculum in more detail, look at how the curriculum and exams should link together, how to change our approach to teaching, and how we provide the right skills to the teaching staff, exam markers and students. It is not a pretty picture, but it needs to change, and it needs to change now. For any international readers this will mostly apply to your educational systems too, but the details and terminology will vary.

The curriculum needs to be ripped up and reinvented. We have to start embedding critical thinking skills across all subjects, right from primary school through to university. I can't cover all subjects, so will focus on English, Maths and Technology. (Please bear in mind that what I say will apply equally to science, geography, economics and the rest.)

First, I want to look at English, but of course feel free to swap that for your native language. In the UK we teach English in two parts, literature and language. Literature explores three well-known books, typically a Shakespeare play, a Dickens novel, and one more, not infrequently *An Inspector Calls* by Priestley. When I was a teenager doing my exams, it was *Romeo and Juliet*, *Great Expectations* and *An Inspector Calls*. Thirty-five years later my son was doing *Macbeth*, *A Christmas Carol*... and *An Inspector Calls* [sigh]. I have often pondered why we haven't moved on from these texts, and I think the answer is simple. It is too difficult and too much effort; teachers know what to expect, and all the supporting books and lesson plans already exist. Shakespeare wrote 400 years ago, Dickens about 170 years ago, and Priestley was knocking on for a century ago. It doesn't seem to matter that there are loads of fantastically well written books out there now that contain more interesting topics and better stories.

English language, the other part of the UK approach, focuses on teaching people how to read, write, and communicate, but we have lost our way with this too. English is now too academic. I called this out earlier, but if you want to measure and score, having black and white answers makes it easier. We have ended up with a system that teaches the formative years all the parts of a structure instead of establishing a wide variation of words and understanding.

We are essentially teaching our children the theory of English, not how to articulate, analyse, and appraise. English, apart from being a strangely structured language, is incredibly versatile and colourful, with thousands of words that can be interchanged. The *Oxford English Dictionary* (OED) suggests that we currently use about 171,000 words and that there are maybe 47,000 additional words that we no longer use. The OED definition of the word 'set' is about thirty-two pages long! English is a wonderful language, but that is not what we are teaching.

Let's leave the academic version of English for Further Education and get back to teaching the wonderful vocabulary, being creative with it, learning how to formulate and articulate, and how to critically appraise text. Let's get critical thinking back in the mix. It is a big shift.

Maths, similarly, is based on a very academic footing. We teach our children about Sine, Cosine, and Tangent, but not how tax works. I fully agree that there is a basic form of mental arithmetic that all children should be taught and that they should know to the point of not even needing to think about it. Multiplication and division, addition and subtraction, fractions and percentages are all critical for day-to-day life. So why do we still teach long division? Teach the children how to work out the answer, not test them on old methods. Today almost everyone has access to a smartphone or computer, certainly in the workplace, so why spend weeks and weeks practicing something like long division, rather than educating them on how to divide in their head, or why, and when you would work out a percentage?

Last of the three is Technology. In the UK at least, Technology is an optional or 'elective' subject. Children are taught how to stay safe online which is useful but considering that we interact with all sorts of technologies every day, be it in a business environment or at home, I fail to see why it is not a core topic. Probably because it is being viewed as a niche academic topic, not a core skill.

Nearly thirty years ago when I first got into computers I learned about all sorts of things, many of which are redundant for the average person, things like the OSI model (Wikipedia) which still features in today's learning. In those thirty years I have used the OSI model maybe once! That said, the children of today consume lots of technology, but with very little understanding of how it connects together and what the dependencies are.

Technology needs to become a core topic, akin to that of Maths and English language but also woven into every subject. In History, use the technology to recount dates and events, and critical thinking to reason, challenge, and create a small thesis on why it worked out as it did. In Science, use the technology to create data sources, and then use it to establish correlations and patterns that critical thinking can be applied to and to establish the next line of investigation.

The focus should shift from rote learning to fostering skills and encouraging students to engage deeply with the content. It is a radical shift, I know, but it is one that is desperately needed. If we allow critical thinking, deep engagement, and wisdom to be replaced with poor literacy, apathy, and cognitive offloading, then we will create a population lacking the necessary tools to challenge misinformation or question government changes that might impact us negatively, and our children will become either unemployable in the new world or will end up in menial roles that have yet to be automated. The curriculum needs to change.

Exams also need to change, and this change needs to be radical. What is our current exam system designed to do? In theory it is there to provide a level playing field for every child or student to be tested against. I have no issue with that per se, but is the playing field level? No, of course not. Those who attend a well-funded establishment or who are fortunate enough to go to a private school will of course fare better than those who don't. The real question here is that, regardless of the quality of your education, the curriculum leads you to a very blinkered exam set-up. I mentioned that exams are typically written by those who have reached the latter part of their educational career, and typically without the input of those who understand the newest technological impacts. This is no longer fit for purpose. We should not be testing future generations on their ability to recall equations, formulae, dates, or events; these things are easy to find using the current technology. We need to teach and test those skills that are dwindling and in decline and if there are areas of underfunding and no access to the technologies, we need to resolve that too.

An example. The current exam format might ask when the slave trade act came into effect in Britain.

A 'new world' exam question might be: 'It is 1807 and you are a plantation owner who relies on slaves. The Slave Trade Act (STA) has come into effect and will be followed by the Slavery Abolition Act (SAA). The ownership of enslaved people will be made illegal in much of the British Empire. Use the following text from the STA and SAA to reason your case for how it will impact your plantation, and how you propose to alter your methods to ensure your operation can still function.'

A longer question with deeper engagement. This approach applies to all subjects in the curriculum. Allow the students to use technology to find facts (or provide the facts, eliminating the need for technology in the exam) and focus the students' effort on formulating their response. Allow the exam system to use technology to check for plagiarism. Then, and yes, I know it would be difficult, but it is not insurmountable, orally test the students on their responses to ensure they understand and can back up their reasoning.

Less dating-agency-style questions, less rote learning, and smaller, more in-depth testing of the ability to justify their reasoning and challenge texts or problems. Maths, English, and Sciences all face the same challenges.

Courses and exams all need to be tied to technology usage by default. Students need to learn how to work with AI and to test and validate its responses. They need to be taught how to analyse current affairs articles from multiple sources. Make them watch the news and then use technology to build a comprehensive picture of what might really have happened. Read modern books with the students and ask them to recreate the ending to bring it more up to date. *Fahrenheit 451* is a great book to do that with.

We have to link the curriculum to teaching, to exams, to technology, to marking, and in order to do that we need technical experts involved at all stages. The UK, or any other country wanting to be a world leader in AI, must make these changes. Failing to change the education systems from top to bottom will result in the creation of a workforce only fit for the most rudimentary of employment, skilled trades, or those that are based around people, like entertainment and leisure.

It is all very well wanting to change the education systems from top to bottom, but how do we upskill the teachers, teaching assistants, exam writers, and those marking them?

Here we face yet another huge challenge. We are asking our entire teaching workforce to become more highly skilled. Do they want to change, and do they understand the need to change? I have known many teachers over the years, and their range in desire to learn and change varies greatly, with the vast majority falling on the side of reluctance. I understand that change, especially of this scale, can be daunting and scary, but they need to play their part too. Let's assume for a moment that the government and the exam boards all agree to change the way we teach, the curriculum, and the exam structures. I'll take a small pause whilst you stop laughing, but now that they are all in agreement, how do we upskill the teaching staff?

In Change Management theory, there are a few stages, but let's look at the first three as without them in place, we are on a hiding to nothing. The Prosci® model for individual change looks at Awareness, Desire, Knowledge, Ability, and

Reinforcement. Awareness is the first stage; do they understand the need to change and the impact of not changing? Are they aware of how this might impact their role as educators of our future workforces? The second stage is around Desire; do they see the benefit in it? Do they see the benefit for themselves and for the students? Stage three is Knowledge; do they know how to use the tools themselves? If any one of those three is lacking there is an issue that needs to be addressed.

It is unlikely that a person will see the benefit of change if they do not understand why the change is needed. If they do not see the benefit of the change, they cannot develop a desire to change, and if there is no desire to change, training becomes a forced issue and potentially pointless. Teachers need to be included in this process so they can have that awareness of and feel like they are part of the future of education. Once they see the benefits of changing from rote learning and memorisation to critical thought and creativity, they can then start to learn for themselves. While it sounds simple and logical, this will be a significant challenge.

Those who mark exams will need to undergo a similar process. Changing from something that was first established in the 1850s to something completely new will be an enormous change for anyone involved in the process.

Applying change management to the entire teaching populace is a big task. Will they all jump at the chance? I very much doubt it. Will many lose their jobs or look at early retirement? I expect so. Is it then fair to ask these teachers to go through all this without suitable recompense? No, I don't think so. Teaching used to be a noble vocation, a calling, but now many feel disillusioned and let down by the government and educational agencies, only there to get students through exams, to improve pass rates, and so on. Teaching will need to return to that noble vocation, with new skills, new ways of thinking, and a revived energy, and with that should come appropriate remuneration.

But what about students, how do we manage the change with them? Here we are in a better position as they have little to no choice in the matter! So long as the expectations and methodology are clear they will have to go along with whatever method of teaching is used. Interestingly, recent discussions with students finds them to be very perceptive of the challenges of the new world versus the current educational approach. I don't think that students will push back on much of this change. They will of course need access to all the tools that are available in business including Gen AI, and for them to access that they need devices, all of which cost money. Who will pay for that?

Now we have added increased salaries, devices, subscriptions, and the reskilling of the entire educational workforce to the national bill. We haven't added the rewriting of the entire curriculum, exam papers, marking or grading policies. You can see why every government is trying to get away with minimal change now.

Teacher training will require significant investment in high-quality professional development, and they will need to be equipped with the necessary skills to teach critical thinking. This will require a fundamental re-orientation from traditional content delivery towards more facilitative and inquiry-based instruction.

Assessment methods must be redesigned to accurately measure critical thinking, and this might include implementing evidence-based assignments, robust class discussions, and performance tasks. It will likely take a shift away from point in time exams to programme-based assessment, including methods such as capstone assessments (as used in the last year of a degree course) where there is a demonstration of mastery of the subject via a mixture of oral and written work, and a more inquisitorial manner to evaluate cognitive skills.

Education is possibly the largest and most complex challenge that we face. Governments all around the world prefer an undereducated populace as they are easier to guide and manipulate. The challenge of reinventing education is so large that no government wishes to tackle it head on. Creating a coalition of curriculum writers, exam boards, course creators, exam markers, educational trusts, and schools, teachers, and assistants, and ensuring they all have sufficient understanding and skills is breathtakingly daunting.

The financial and time investment required to achieve it would be astronomical, with new devices, subscriptions, and training for all. Even if this became a government priority it would take years to implement, and those years will result in the technology taking hold before educational reform even gains traction.

That time gap will result in a generation or two of children lacking the skills required to live and operate in a world with AI. Businesses will be forced to bridge that gap and, in general, most businesses struggle with the concept of actively investing in existing resources let alone bridging the gap left by education.

Chapter 25 – Societal

Societal change worries me greatly as I don't know if it can be fixed. The challenge in business is big, the challenge in education is huge, but the challenge in society is enormous. Trying to change the way that billions of people think feels like an insurmountable task.

Creating a society that understands issues, accepts different viewpoints and values, and that can live in the world today is a lovely concept. A society like that is built on a few core values.

Societal Core Value One: Actively listening in conversations. Really focus on hearing and understanding the other person's perspective, rather than just waiting for your turn to speak. Pay attention to the words, tone, and body language, and ask clarifying questions to ensure you've understood correctly. This very simple act goes to validate the other person's feelings and experiences as they have 'been heard'.

Societal Core Value Two: Seek out different perspectives. Be open to being wrong about your views or beliefs. Intentionally seek out people from different backgrounds, with different beliefs and life experiences from your own. This could be through reading books, watching documentaries, or, even better, having genuine conversations with a human being. Everyone is unique and has their own story, everyone knows something you don't, and the broader your engagement with other cultures and races, the more you will learn. This value helps to break down stereotypes and fosters empathy.

Thirty years ago, Darryl Davis, a musician, befriended a member of the Klu Klux Klan (KKK) and they bonded over the same love of music. The challenge was that Darryl is black. Since that encounter, Darryl has been befriending members of the KKK and claims to have encouraged over two hundred members to drop their robes. Darryl said in a 2017 interview, 'I decided to go around the country and sit down with Klan leaders and Klan members to find out: How can you hate me when you don't even know me? The best thing you do is you study up on the subject as much as you can. I went in armed, not with a weapon, but with knowledge. I knew as much about the Klan, if not more than many of the Klan people that I interviewed. When they see that you know about their organisation, their belief system, they respect you. Whether they like you or not, they respect the fact that you've done your homework. Just like any good salesman, you want a return visit, and they recognized that I'd done my homework, which allowed me to come back again. That began to chip away at their ideology because when two enemies are talking, they're not fighting. It's when the talking ceases that the ground becomes fertile for violence. If you spend five minutes with your worst enemy – it doesn't have to be about race, it could be about anything... you will find that you both have something in common. As you build upon those commonalities, you're forming a relationship and as you build about that relationship, you're forming a friendship.

That's what would happen. I didn't convert anybody. They saw the light and converted themselves.'

Societal Core Value Three: Showing vulnerability. Sharing your own struggles and moments of uncertainty can create a safe space for others to do the same. When you're open about your imperfections, you give others permission to be human too. This builds trust and shows that it's OK not to have all the answers, which can be incredibly unifying.

Societal Core Value Four: Educate yourself on the systemic issues. Gaining understanding of the historical and societal factors that contribute to inequality and division is crucial. Read about issues like social injustice, economic disparities, and mental health challenges. Knowledge empowers you to advocate for change beyond individual interactions. That knowledge can then be used to support policies and initiatives in creating a more equitable foundation for everyone.

How do we go about tackling societal change? We know that fixing the education system will be the foundation for long-term change, but we also need to try to re-educate and fix society today. And who is this magical 'we' I speak of? It is us, normal people; you, me, friends, colleagues, readers, as many as possible to turn the tide.

We start by raising awareness of the issue, encouraging curiosity and the active cultivation of critical thinking; this must transcend work, educational, societal, racial, gender, and familial spheres if we are to stand any chance. The creation of divisions in society must be stopped; we are not each other's enemies. But the fuelling of racism, fear, and xenophobia is a very powerful tool for those who do seek power. Division is not resolved through exclusion.

Rebuilding critical thinking skills is no small task amongst those who want to learn, let alone with those who don't see why they need to change their ways, or even want to. It requires us as a society to cultivate new, foundational habits, habits that include asking simple questions about information that we encounter, actively evaluating evidence, and considering more than our own perspective, even when, or especially if, they differ from our own. We must learn to challenge our own assumptions and biases and deliberately seek out alternative perspectives and viewpoints. We have to learn to identify the presence of biases, fallacies, and loaded narratives, but even more we must try and encourage this kind of thinking in others.

How do people react when you tell them they're wrong? If you directly counter or contradict someone's beliefs, views, or what they consider to be fact it is likely to result in argument, and that rarely achieves anything.

Helping our fellow citizens to see that there are other views and perspectives, that fact is not always what is put in front of them, and that maybe broadening their horizons and understanding of a topic would be worthwhile, might result in a different conclusion.

Either way, leading a person to re-evaluate their existing beliefs is far more effective than telling them they are wrong. That only serves to build resentment.

Change Management theory states that people are unlikely to alter their ways unless they truly understand why it is important, so we start there. We need to help people understand the impact and perils of drawing conclusions with insufficient information. Once there's an understanding and realisation it will allow their brains to start thinking about what they read or see in a different way and will help them to start establishing fact from fiction. Only then will their way of thinking start to change.

Step one is therefore incredibly simple: we change the thinking of the whole of society and make the entire world aware of the problem. Easy!

This will be a monumental struggle, especially when you consider that to create that awareness and to open people's eyes to the problem we need to use the same apps, campaigns, and mechanisms that are having a negative impact on them, or that are being used to condition them. Yes, we will need to use social media to create an engaging campaign that will gain traction using all the same technologies, games, and psychological methods.

A campaign that just tells people to fact check is not likely to engage or succeed; those whose thinking is open to that kind of campaign are most likely not the target audience. That means we need to resort to something catchy, distracting, viral, and maybe even game-like, that builds both awareness and desire. It will have to appeal to all demographics; the young and old, wealthy and less well off, it will need to be available in multiple languages, attract different cultures, and of course, be available across multiple different platforms. See, it is not that bad… oh yes, and it will need to run for many years!

Who has the power to be able to pull something like this off? Me? Oh, dear no, I could certainly have a go, but it would take a very long time, and any campaign of that scale would likely be buried by new content almost immediately, or if I were sceptical, potentially even through suppression. Volume is an issue: Facebook has about three billion monthly active users, Instagram has two billion, and Snapchat nearly a billion. The chances of one voice succeeding in that environment is slim to say the least.

Besides, I'm someone who the vast majority of the world has never heard of. Why would anyone take note of me? It needs to have gravitas and a tone of authority about it. It must be something promoted by governments and that tech firms, celebrities, influencers, and us, all agree is an issue and look to help address, as many people with any kind of following, platform, influence, power, or reach will need to be involved.

Will this happen? I very much doubt it. I can't see those in power or control wishing to undertake such a massive challenge, especially if they do not see, or do not want to see, the problem. I do not see the tech firms caring enough about it when it sits counter to what they want to achieve, and I do not believe that celebrities and influencers are even aware of this being an issue.

Now that we have practically ruled out official help from those parties mentioned above, step one, awareness, will fall to us as local societies and a collection of individuals. Local, these days, can of course mean both your geographically local community and your virtual world, but it is us who need to become the real-world protagonists. Creating an anti-dystopian campaign will take numbers. In the novels there is typically a lone voice questioning their own existence, we however will need millions of people questioning and challenging the establishments and status quo.

It is 'The Power of One'; the theory that one person's actions can change the future and that those actions can impact the lives of many. If I spread the word to all my contacts, friends, and acquaintances one by one, and convince them that we are already in the early stages of a dystopian world, that we need to re-evaluate what we are being told and how we are being manipulated; and then you do the same, and they do the same, then eventually there will be a groundswell of realisation. Two to the power of ten is just over a thousand people, a good start; however, two to the power of twenty is over a million people.

We know that we cannot rely on government, media, or tech companies to make this happen for us. Groundswell movements represent a powerful tool for change as they are bottom-up, often spontaneous and born of frustration. These groundswell movements have historically relied on traditional methods of organisation, such as house meetings and door-to-door campaigns, and have very much been on a local level, but the digital age has introduced new mechanisms for mobilisation. Modern social movements can stir up large media coverage and potentially go viral. Social media in this case is a tool for spreading awareness, but it will not create a movement for you.

The Black Lives Matter campaign is a very good example of what can be achieved. It began with a Facebook post and hashtag, and while that post might not have had an impact, it succeeded because of the dedication to creating a grassroots movement. The movement gained momentum beyond the world of social media when it transitioned into genuine, real-world connections. Local supporters and groups arranged demonstrations fostering genuine connections among people. In sharing personal accounts and showing empathy the movement converted into a campaign for change.

The digital world can be leveraged to provide a platform for awareness and a starting point for connection, but the real power comes in the shift from the digital realm into a tangible, human based conversation.

Step two is to start to correct behaviour. It is now no longer sufficient to simply realise that someone is wrong; we must challenge those spreading misinformation, regardless of whether it is through motivation or ignorance, to validate their information or source. It might not correct the misinformation at that point in time, but as most of us have access to the internet we can fact check on the spot, search for the correct information, and have a discussion.

I often compare the correction of human behaviour to that of the behavioural training of dogs. If you could ask a dog what the time was, they would say it was 'now' as they have no concept of what happened last week. They live entirely in the moment. So, if you want to correct their behaviour, you need to do it there and then. It does not need to be aggressive, but enough so they know the behaviour is not OK. Sitting a dog down and telling them that what they did last Wednesday was out of order will get you absolutely nowhere. In this regard humans are no different. If you want to correct human behaviour it is best to do so when it happens. If you have a political leader or representative, work leader, or friend, who says something misleading or clearly incorrect, ask them where they got the information from, and if possible, present them with new, validated information. It is not an easy or comfortable thing to do by any means, but the issue of non-correction is critical at all levels; local, national and international; especially in the world of politics.

Leaders and party members across the world frequently make untrue claims and openly lie about statistics, situations, and causes. Many journalists and reporters seem to have fallen into the trap of just reporting the sensational headlines on the principle that 'bad news sells', rather than question the supplied information at the point it is said. As mentioned before, if the misinformation is quoted in public, then regardless of any potential future retraction or correction the damage has already been done. It is typically the first news that wins, not the truth. The media becomes filled with what was said, not what was apologised for or corrected. If that is the case, is it worth trying to fight? Yes, we need to hold people to account regardless. This is not something that we should allow to go unchallenged. It need not be aggressive or confrontational, but it needs to happen.

If I am presented with new information that is contrary to my current understanding, and it seems to make sense and 'stacks up', then I like to think that I will change my mind on that situation or belief. Unfortunately, this seems to be increasingly not the case with the wider populace; you, as a reader of this book may well be of a similar mindset to me, however, when dealing with those who already have a disinterest in fact finding, deep engagement and critical thinking, the task becomes much more difficult.

Step one is awareness, step two is active correction, step three needs to be targeted at parents. This will not be a quick fix as the parents in scope are probably also unaware of the issue and might well be part of the problem; yet we will be asking them to help change their children's thought processes.

What can parents do? Teach their children to question what they see, read, and hear. 'The five whys' is a good place to start. Why? Why? Why? Why? Why? or Who, What, Why, When and How? And to keep going until there is a suitable answer.

Why do you think that? What have you read? Where did you see it? Who published it? Who does it benefit? Can you find the same information anywhere else? Can you find anything official to back up the claim? Who do they work for? What do they get out of it? Why now?

One of the biggest issues with this step is that it relies on the current general populace suddenly changing their ways and teaching their children to question things. Even if we start to correct the parents, and let's say that works, does that provide them with the skills to then redirect how their children think? No, but does that mean it is not worth trying? Also no; we must try. Only by teaming up and encouraging people, changing attitudes, education, and making critical thinking a default response will we stand any chance.

It is theoretically possible to provide a free educational course online for all people, not just parents, but those courses typically face low uptake especially when the target audience sees no reason to change. In the UK in the 1970s there were Public Information Films. They taught us about stranger danger, crossing the road, electrical safety, drowning, riding bicycles, burns, fires, and rabies and, in fairness, it scarred most children to the point where the advice is still vividly remembered today. 'Remember kids, electricity kills!' They were extremely effective. Over forty years later I put out a domestic fire using the same 'damp tea towel' technique learned from those little films when I was a kid. Brilliant. These things work when done properly. It would of course need to be repeated frequently on multiple media streams for many years for it to take root in a generational mindset in the same kind of way.

There are many tools out there to help. There are books on critical thinking, thinking clearly, and other mechanisms like 'argument mapping' which uses a visual representation of an argument to help to analyse and identify any weak points in reasoning. A good book is *The Art of Thinking Clearly* by Rolf Dobelli (Dobeli, 2014) which lists 99 ways in which our thinking becomes flawed by bias and fallacies. It doesn't harp on in too much depth but instead demonstrates how these traits impact the choices we make. Engaging in structured activities like debates allows individuals to defend opposing viewpoints through thoughtful discussion without the pressure of having to conclude with a 'right' or 'wrong' answer.

For many, the world is becoming more like a soap opera than something you live and exist in. It is watched through screens, the characters are not real people that you know or can relate to, and it is not something that you experience in person unless one of the storylines impacts you directly.

This is amplified further when it comes to interacting with other humans from behind a keyboard. It seems to afford many an additional layer of protection, allowing them to say what they like without repercussion. I was taught that if you wouldn't say something to someone's face, then don't say it. If I am rude to someone directly, and they don't like it, I might even feel the physical repercussion in the form of a fist to the face. There are no such consequences online.

This dehumanisation goes far deeper than ever before, and with the creation of deepfake apps that are freely available, it is easy for almost anyone to create fake images of anyone they like, in very compromising, sexually explicit or illegal situations. Laura Bates' book *The New Age of Sexism* (Bates, 2025) covers this topic incredibly well and in great detail. People have the ability to dehumanise, embarrass, and destroy the lives of anyone they fancy at the touch of a button.

Whilst creating new forms of disconnection, we can use technologies for good and to break down traditional barriers such as the lack of accessibility for those with disabilities. Inclusion is not just about providing access to a gadget or the internet, it is about ensuring that everyone has the skills, training, and support required to thrive in this new world. It is a double-edged sword. It creates a digital divide and fragmentation of society, especially marginalising younger generations from low-income communities who lack access to devices and training. On the other hand, strategic partnerships between tech companies and nonprofits *could* leverage technology to empower these same young people, providing them with laptops, coding skills, and mentorship programs that can transform their academic performance and open doors to future career opportunities.

The ultimate challenge we are presented with is reclaiming the world as a real place with real people, people with feelings and empathy. Our personal lives have been split into the real world and the online world and there is a danger of slipping too far to the point where we lose a sense of real priorities.

There is no external enemy to be defeated, the technology companies and apps are not the problem per se, but we are fighting an insidious, self-imposed mode of existence where apathy, disengagement, and intellectual decline are the weapons we are using against ourselves. We are struggling to maintain our individual agency in the face of a constant, seductive pull toward virtual appeasement. When this happens it leaves the door wide open for those with desires on power to walk right in and seize it.

Fixing society requires a unified and simultaneous effort. At the personal level we need to cultivate critical thinking and intellectual reflection. In the family it is about having the courage to break habits and patterns, and to rebuild resilience and real-world social skills. In the community it is about using grassroots action and building genuine, trust-filled relationships.

This decline is not irreversible, but it requires an intentional return to tangible, human connections. The constant stream of appeasement, distraction, and manipulation has successfully created a population that, whilst not openly oppressed, is far too disengaged to recognise its own intellectual and social erosion. Something that is completely and uncomfortably in line with the narrative of *Fahrenheit 451*.

Chapter 26 – Political & Judicial

A growing sense of apathy is not an inherent trait of a populace, it is a predictable outcome when addressable barriers, such as a general sense of powerlessness, poor leadership, or a lack of investment in education and society, lead people to feel their needs are being ignored. Modern politics certainly has the ability to make you feel insignificant; that you're just another part of a massive system which exists to serve others and which you can do little to influence. It is why politicians who purport to want to reclaim the country and services do so regardless of whether or not their intentions match their words.

I have combined the political and judicial scenes into one: law is after all made through government. We need a radical change in how governments and law-makers operate. They are unable to keep up with the rate of change today, and this will only become more prevalent if nothing is done.

The Civil Service Departments which set the agenda for Schools, Justice and Law, Health and Social Care, Transport, etc., are all controlled by the political party in power. Each party will be driving their own agenda and stands to be replaced every five years at election time.

This is a major issue: how can you build continuity based on that principle? How can you set long-term goals that aren't going to be trashed by the next party in power? How can you put in place a policy which will need a decade to truly take effect when there is pressure to demonstrate 'success' before the next election?

The phrase 'the government in power' smells bad; it should not be about power, it should be about serving the country and its people. Politics has become about power when it should be about service. It is a ridiculous system that is based on one party having sufficient power to topple the other and allows the opportunity to undo any potentially good works in progress. I have no desire to become a political commentator, but it feels to me like a system that is destined to screw any country over.

Regarding English law, things have been a bit bumpy over the years. The first use of the term Parliament dates to 1236CE. Gradually over the centuries it created the two-party system that we have today. There are of course more than two parties, but currently the numbers of seats held by the other parties are significantly lower. Our current system is built on foundations laid down when Henry VIII was on the throne, people lived on pottage, and it was OK to throw your excrement out of the window. It's a system founded some three hundred years before we decided it was OK to start burning women as witches because they looked a bit odd, acted funny, or stood up for themselves. It is not a disastrous system, and the UK government is still preferable to many alternatives, however it is now the source of many of our issues, and as we are seeing, it has become easier to blame minorities or immigrants than to take responsibility.

One thing to make clear is that there is enough wealth in most developed countries to provide great services, support for all who need it, and have wonderful infrastructure. That is not in doubt, but have you ever noticed that when there apparently is no money for schools or roads, there is for war? It is a centuries old playbook.

The relationship between the government and corporate entities needs to be addressed. It is becoming increasingly noticeable and intermingled with ethical lines becoming very blurred. Corporate lobbying, where companies and associations attempt to influence policymakers, is now a multi-billion-pound industry in its own right, and whilst legal, it creates a sense of obligation and unspoken favouritism within the political system. This allows those with sufficient buying power to 'shape' legislation in their favour, often leading to policies that protect corporate profits at the expense of public welfare or environmental protection.

In the UK it is not uncommon to hear political funding and lobbying being criticised for being easy to circumvent and this raises serious questions over who is really pulling the strings. A system where economic power dictates or defines political outcomes is a dangerous one. It is easy to see it in action; there are lots of companies and associations at it (for example energy companies, banks, the NRA in the US), and it is all brushed neatly into being OK because it is 'lobbying'. Giving it a name seems to have legitimised the process; having a name makes it all above board and nothing to worry about. I challenge that. No business should have the power to buy the allegiance of a member of parliament through 'political donations' or any other kind of reward, holidays, entertainment, gifts, etc. If business is allowed too close to the government it creates a fertile environment that is ripe for abuse.

We should also be questioning the suitability of MPs having second jobs or financial interests in companies that serve as a conflict of interest. If you look at the UK during the pandemic, the number of contracts handed out to MPs, relatives or where they were a stakeholder is crazy. MPs with interests in private medical service providers have been found to vote against funding the NHS properly. I wonder why? This is tightly linked to the 'revolving door' phenomenon where individuals move between high-level government positions and lucrative jobs in the private sector. Senior politicians, civil servants, and military personnel often transition to roles as consultants, lobbyists, or board members for the very companies they once regulated or awarded contracts to. This practice raises serious questions about potential conflicts of interest and raises concerns that current officials may make decisions based on the prospect of their future employment, while former officials can exploit their insider knowledge and personal connections to secure favourable treatment. This is corruption. It doesn't matter how you dress it up to legitimise it, it is corruption in some form or other. The government is supposed to be there to serve the people, not business, and the two do not mix well.

Addressing these issues will again require comprehensive reforms. Complete transparency in political funding is paramount, and at the time it takes place, not one or two years later. The lobbying industry must be more tightly regulated, with mandatory publicly visible registers detailing every meeting between a politician and a lobbyist, including the topics discussed and the outcomes. And the revolving door should be closed, maybe through the creation of enforced waiting periods for former public officials before they can take up roles in their relevant industries, and the formation of a truly independent ethics commission with real power to investigate and prosecute. We need to ensure that these reforms are more than just a performative gesture.

In addition to this is the relationship between government and the large tech and big data firms. These companies are getting too close to, and too cosy with, the government. But it doesn't stop there, they are also getting too close to the public data held on us all; something I have serious concerns over. There are a few well-established organisations that are run by people who I believe hold very questionable and unethical views, and they are getting ever closer to gaining control of the data held about you and me. This will of course always be officially denied as there will be 'checks and measures' in place to ensure the integrity of the data, but I will remain firmly on the side of scepticism for now. After all, the checks and measures are only as good as the mechanisms and the people doing the checking and measuring.

Social media also has its part to play in politics. It has changed how the political scene operates, and it has developed into a breeding ground for misinformation, polarisation, and dehumanisation. It is a form of politics that plays on people's emotions, prioritising engagement over accurate content or truth. Promoting emotionally charged or sensational content has created an environment where disinformation, conspiracy theories, and divisive narratives can spread quickly.

When this kind of politics is combined with filter bubbles, echo chambers and affirmation bias, reasoned debate becomes nearly impossible. People become more entrenched in their pre-existing views, and they lose the ability to empathise with opposing viewpoints, leading to the increased political polarisation that we are seeing today. This division of the country into a form of tribal state sees any shared national identity replaced with a collection of fragmented, often hostile sub-groups.

Creating a plan to address these things is not straightforward, as you can imagine. Any regulation of social media needs to balance free speech with public safety.

In the UK, the concept of free speech is primarily protected under Article 10 of the Human Rights Act 1998. This act incorporates the European Convention on Human Rights into UK law. Article 10 states that everyone has the right to freedom of expression, which includes the freedom to hold opinions and to 'receive and impart information and ideas without interference by public authority'.

But free speech is not absolute. UK law allows for restrictions when necessary to protect other people's rights and public interests. The common limitations on free speech in the UK are defamation, hate speech, incitement to violence or terrorism, public order offences, and national security.

These restrictions must be 'prescribed by law' and 'necessary in a democratic society'.

Any reforms would need to focus on holding platforms and people accountable for the content they promote, rather than what is merely posted. This could include requiring platforms to provide robust mechanisms for users to report disinformation, or through the automatic labelling and withdrawal of political statements that are clearly untrue. None of this would be easy to determine.

If holding platforms, organisations, companies, and people accountable for what is presented were to go ahead in any form, then the supporting legislation and judiciary system would also require change. Our legal and justice systems were designed for a slower-moving world. For some time they have struggled to keep pace with the complexities of the digital age, but with the current direction of travel I would say it is about to become almost ineffective. The pace of technological change far outstrips the speed of legislative action. Whilst new technologies are rapidly transforming society, the laws governing them are either non-existent or woefully outdated. This lag allows a legal vacuum to be created, enabling tech companies and others to operate with minimal oversight and accountability. Laws governing data privacy and intellectual property are constantly having to play catch-up with technologies that collect and use personal data. This slow-moving, reactive approach to lawmaking will have a significant part to play in our march towards a dystopian world. A slow, bureaucratic, and out of touch justice system will lose the trust and respect of the public, and a justice system that cannot or will not effectively protect its citizens is, by definition, failing its core function.

For the legal system to really work in this new age, it will require the creation of a permanent, cross-party parliamentary committee that is dedicated to identifying and future-proofing legislation against technological change, a greater investment in training to ensure judges and prosecutors are well versed in technological and digital issues, and a public-facing dialogue about the future of law to build consensus and public trust.

The government is also responsible for setting out the plans for education and despite its unquestionable importance, educational reform often faces strong resistance both politically and societally.

If we fail to address and act on these issues, we risk reaching further into a society that shows significant dystopian traits. The elite and wealthy go unchecked, regulations are weak, leadership is poor, manipulation and misinformation are high, and the populace are malleable through the lack of education and skills. Social media is a pit of disinformation and lies, and keeps the populace distracted and divided, making any united resistance near impossible; and a slow, outdated justice system goes to reinforce the belief that power lies beyond accountability.

All these things go to consolidate immense power to the few.

An uneducated and disenfranchised populace are unable to challenge the status quo, and mass unemployment is a breeding ground for social unrest. This is a future where any idea of a fair and just society is replaced by a system that serves only a privileged few.

All is not lost though; the alternative is that we actively confront these challenges. A political model that is based on radical transparency, away from the two-party system, where one vote is one vote, and where political power is no longer tied so tightly to corporate wealth.

We can create a digital landscape that unites, rather than divides, through the promotion of critical thinking, and holding platforms and people accountable. Yes, it requires an agile legal framework to ensure that no one is above the law, regardless of their power or position. This is a path of deliberate reform, and it is down to us, the people, to demand change.

Part 6 – Conclusion

Chapter 27 – Prepare Yourself

Time to wrap up. We need to be objective about how far we are from the reality of a full, real-world dystopia. I have shared my observations and thoughts, but they are just that, they are MY observations and thoughts. This part of the book introduces the concept of the Dystopian Delta Index. It is very simple: what are the signs of a dystopia, and how well established are they?

It is a reasonably effective indicator of how close we are to living in a full dystopian society. It is not based on science and there is no complicated algorithm crunching data. It is a subjective visualisation of your opinion.

I then want to talk about what happens if we don't address all the issues I have discussed. How might society pan out when all these components come together. It'll be blunt, so make sure you have suitably fortifying refreshment to hand; or if you are British, maybe a cup of tea.

Finally, I will cover off what we, you, and society in general can do to help: how we can become the protagonists of our own dystopian environment.

Chapter 28 – Are We There Yet?

How on earth do you start to work out how close we are to being in a dystopian environment? This is something I have given a lot of thought to recently. After multiple attempts and trials I have come up with the Dystopian Delta Index.

Originally this was a huge set of questions that covered all the aspects talked about in this book. This presented a challenge as people don't want to sit and answer that many questions, so I've condensed them into a handful of deep questions that probe into how you feel about the world, politics, planet, and so on. It is of course subjective; someone wealthy living in London might have a very different view of the world to someone living in a less affluent part of the country and who is struggling to get by each week.

Dystopian Delta Index

Each question comes with an explanation and a scoring guide, once you have reviewed the information, score it between 1 and 10 and move to the next question. There is one question each on Trust, Agency, Truth, Apathy, Dehumanisation, Innovation, Environment, Economic Inequality, Critical Thinking, and Civic Engagement.

Please answer as honestly as possible. Once you have completed the questions and scored them accordingly, we will look at how we should interpret them.

Question 1: Trust

> To what degree are the primary sources of public information and governance perceived as aligned with the common good for the people, versus self-interest or organisational agenda?

This question probes the public's perception of institutional motivation and considers the decline in confidence in both government and mass media. The question is whether the public views these institutions as having integrity or as being 'corrupt' and 'biased':

Scoring Guidance:

1–3: Broad, bipartisan trust in institutions, which are perceived as transparent and acting in the public interest. The public believes institutions are a reliable source of facts.

4–6: Trust is low but not yet at a critical level. Partisan divides are visible, but a significant portion of the population remains neutral or holds moderate views. There are clear, actionable paths to restoring confidence.

7–10: Trust is at a historic low, with the majority of the public viewing institutions as 'corrupt' and 'biased'. Perceptions are deeply polarised along partisan lines, with a near-total loss of confidence in reporting objectivity.

Question 2: Agency

How much influence do people feel they have over the systems (technological, bureaucratic, or corporate) that govern their daily lives?

This question seeks to measure the sense of individual control. It is not about political participation, but about the tangible feeling of having a say in your own environment.

Scoring Guidance:

1–3: A large majority of individuals feel they have a significant say in how technology is adopted and how bureaucracy impacts their lives. This contributes to high job and life satisfaction.

4–6: A significant minority of the population expresses concern about technology adoption, leading to dissatisfaction. A growing number feel that their choices are inconsequential.

7–10: The majority of the population feel that their lives are governed by powerful, opaque systems that are incomprehensible to them and to which they have surrendered control.

Question 3: Truth

Is there a shared and accepted baseline of objective reality, or are there multiple and competing 'realities' in circulation?

This question looks at the state of a society's information ecosystem and the public's ability to engage with factual information.

Scoring Guidance:

1–3: Whilst misinformation exists, a shared, factual baseline is broadly accepted. The public relies on a diversity of sources and demonstrates a willingness to engage with information that challenges their existing beliefs.

4–6: The public's trust in truth is fragmented. Misinformation spreads faster than truth, but there are still broadly accepted, credible sources of information that are trusted across the political spectrum.

7–10: A shared reality has collapsed. The public is divided into competing information bubbles that reinforce existing biases, making reasoned debate impossible. Algorithms and social media have trapped users, who are more likely to accept information that matches their existing beliefs.

Question 4: Apathy

> When faced with public suffering or injustice, is the prevailing societal response one of active civic engagement or passive desensitisation?

This question aims to understand the level of societal apathy, which is a key psychological and sociological response to powerlessness. It assesses whether a society's members are civically engaged or have become indifferent to the plight of others.

Scoring Guidance:

1–3: The people exhibit high levels of civic engagement and collective action, as seen with social movements and volunteerism. They believe in their ability to make a difference and actively respond to public suffering and injustice.

4–6: Civic engagement is present but inconsistent. Political apathy is a growing issue, particularly among younger generations, but key issues can still motivate public action and voter turnout.

7–10: Societal apathy is a pervasive feature. The public feels a sense of powerlessness and desensitisation, with a lack of interest or concern for social issues. Citizens believe that a problem is 'not their problem'.

Question 5: Dehumanisation

Is a person's value primarily defined by their utility to the state or a dominant system, or by their inherent dignity and individuality?

This question asks whether a society upholds the inherent dignity of its citizens or reduces them to cogs in a machine, measured by conformity and productive output.

Scoring Guidance:

1–3: Society celebrates and protects individuality and self-expression. A person's value is tied to their inherent dignity, and the pursuit of a well-lived life is considered a virtue.

4–6: There is pressure for conformity. Certain groups are marginalised, and the concept of individuality is threatened by societal or corporate norms.

7–10: Society enforces uniform expectations. People's value is judged by their utility to an external system, such as a corporation or the state. Dissent is suppressed, and individuality is perceived as a threat.

Question 6: Innovation

> Is technological and scientific advancement primarily aimed at solving complex human problems, or at control, efficiency, and surveillance at the cost of human agency?

This question examines the purpose and effect of a society's technological infrastructure.

Scoring Guidance:

1–3: Technology is seen as a tool for human empowerment, with its development guided by ethical frameworks that prioritise human well-being. It is transparent and accessible to a wide audience.

4–6: Technology is a double-edged sword, providing benefits while also raising concerns about privacy and control. There is a gap in technology adoption, but efforts are being made to address it.

7–10: Society is controlled by technology. Advancement is primarily aimed at eroding privacy, gaining power, and conditioning people. Citizens have surrendered control to technology.

Question 7: Environment

Is the natural world viewed as an integral part of human well-being, or as a resource?

This question asks whether society has a sustainable, reciprocal relationship with nature or has abused it to a point of no return.

Scoring Guidance:

1–3: The natural world is valued and protected as essential for human health and well-being. Efforts are made to ensure a healthy environment for all.

4–6: Environmental degradation is a concern, but it is not yet cataclysmic. There is a sense of urgency, but action is inconsistent or politically polarised.

7–10: The natural world is in crisis and environmental disaster is a reality, with the widespread pollution of air and water. The environment is viewed as a nothing more than a resource or an obstacle to be conquered, rather than as an integral part of the ecosystem.

Question 8: Economic Equality

How tightly is a person's life expectancy, health, and well-being tied to their socioeconomic position?

This question seeks to understand systemic inequity. It asks whether health and well-being follow a social gradient and whether economic disparity has created a rigid hierarchy.

Scoring Guidance:

1–3: Health and well-being are broadly accessible, with minimal variation across socioeconomic lines. Society prioritises reducing health disparities as an explicit goal.

4–6: There are noticeable differences in health and life expectancy tied to socioeconomic position, but they are not yet extreme. There is a clear correlation between higher income and access to services.

7–10: Society is defined by a deep and widening gap in health outcomes and life expectancy between the rich and the poor. A person's quality of life is largely determined by their socioeconomic position.

Question 9: Critical Thinking

> Are critical thinking and information literacy seen as essential skills for public life, or are they devalued in favour of quick, emotional, and self-reinforcing responses?

This question asks about society's ability to resist the pervasive effects of misinformation.

Scoring Guidance:

1–3: Critical thinking is a valued skill taught in educational institutions and widely applied in public discourse. People can evaluate evidence, analyse arguments, and make rational decisions based on sound information.

4–6: There is a growing deficit of critical thinking skills, leading to an increased susceptibility to misinformation and cognitive biases. The populace is vulnerable to emotional manipulation.

7–10: The majority of the populace lacks the ability to analyse arguments and evaluate evidence. Critical thinking is devalued in favour of reactive, emotional, and self-reinforcing decisions, which are easily manipulated by technology.

Question 10 – Civic Engagement

Is public participation primarily a means of exercising individual power and shaping society, or is it a prescribed ritual managed by external systems?

This question assesses the nature of public participation. It distinguishes between meaningful engagement and 'Performative Action' or the performance of empty rituals.

Scoring Guidance:

1–3: Public participation is a robust and meaningful process that allows individuals to feel a sense of purpose and to exercise their power. It is seen as a way to identify and address issues of public concern.

4–6: Participation is inconsistent, with many people feeling that their vote or voice has little impact. Civic involvement is becoming more ritualistic and less a driver of tangible change.

7–10: Public participation is a managed, empty ritual. Bureaucracy or other external systems control the process, and individuals feel they have no real power. The people view participation as a meaningless gesture, fuelling widespread apathy and disengagement.

Scoring

How do we interpret the scores?

A score of 1 to 3 raises no concern whatsoever; it is not an area that needs any real focus for change. 4 and 5 are often an indicator that you're not sure about it, you haven't really given it any real consideration or that you feel fairly neutral about the topic. 6 is an indication that there are issues and that, in your opinion, we are seeing the early signs of dystopia. 7 and upwards are and should be treated as a major concern and viewed as issues we need to address. Anything that scores 10 should see us out on the streets, fighting with all we have for immediate change.

If you take the average score over the ten questions, you will get a general idea of the overall state of things. 6 should be viewed as worrying, and an average of 7.5 or above should be raising alarm bells as, by this point, it will be very difficult, if not impossible, to turn the tide.

My own views at the point of writing are:

Trust	- - - - - - 7 - - -
Agency	- - - - - 6 - - - -
Truth	- - - - - 6 - - - -
Apathy	- - - - - - - 8 - -
Dehumanisation	- - - - - - 7 - - -
Innovation	- - - - - 6 - - - -
Environment	- - - - - - - 8 - -
Economic Inequality	- - - - - - 7 - - -
Critical Thinking	- - - - - - - 8 - -
Civic Engagement	- - - - 5 - - - - -

What does that tell us about my thinking?

I'm not overly concerned about Civic Engagement, I think the people will rally if things get too uncomfortable, I have some faith in that.

Agency, Truth, and Innovation are all points for concern as I see them being in the early stages of a dystopian society. I am especially concerned about the manipulation of Truth for the gain of the few.

I am very concerned about the lack of trust, dehumanisation, and economic equality we are seeing.

More and more I see trust being eroded in the political sphere as politicians break promises with increasingly blatant lies being spread with little to no recourse. We frequently see messaging about immigrants blocking NHS services, and so on. Statistics show this to be untrue, but it goes to show I cannot trust the traditional media, social media, or social commentary. The growing number of people who are believing things that just aren't legitimate worries me considerably.

Dehumanisation can be easily seen through the right-wing politics in play, along with genuine atrocities like the genocide in Gaza, etc. Large sections of the populace don't seem to be bothered about what is happening; they are aware, but it is more akin to watching a TV drama, as if the people involved aren't real somehow.

I hold grave concerns over the inequality in the world. I'm not naive enough to think that everyone should have an equal share, but the gap is too large. Those people and businesses that are in the millions, billions, and trillions don't pay much tax because the rules allow them not to. If taxes are to be paid effectively to fund central government, then those tax loopholes need to be closed. If you want to blame anyone, rather than blaming those who can afford to employ clever accountants to utilise all the loopholes, blame those who create the tax laws. The poor are getting poorer and the rich, richer. Those who have will generally be fine with medical and dental care, food, transport, education for their children; they will have access to the latest devices and tooling to ensure good access to media and learning. The have-nots will fall further and further behind in all of those aspects, and this will start to create the fracture in society that is so often portrayed in dystopian novels and movies.

With regards to Apathy, Environment, and Critical Thinking, I suspect these are already too well established to reverse.

Apathy is rife: I look through all sorts of social media and real-world situations and see people shrugging off extremely serious issues as if they either have no energy or desire to get involved or genuinely don't care. Performative action, which was seen so much in the displaying of Ukrainian flags on social media when Russia invaded, or the Tricolore when Charlie Hebdo was shot in Paris in 2015, is starting to die away. Society is becoming immune to terrible things.

The planet is still being fought over for religious or resource purposes, and we treat it like dirt. There is a wonderful piece from Conservation International (International, 2014) where Julia Roberts voices Mother Nature. Its message? People need the planet; the planet does not need people. We would do very well to remember that. The more we damage and destroy our planet, the closer we will get to the planet not being able to sustain our greed or provide for us.

Critical Thinking is the most important element for me. In general, people are not applying critical thinking. But everything that I have discussed in this book, from the very start, can be countered by critical thinking.

If we teach all ages to think critically, then we will collectively start to challenge politics and politicians, we will question what we see on social media, we will fact check, we will see others as humans and not the source of issues, we will stop blindly accepting information, and we will stop following the herd. We would challenge what our children are being taught, we would challenge what we are being told on TV, we would become wiser, we would be more active, we would be able to filter the truth from the crap, we would seek deeper engagement in topics. We would be the people we need to be in the modern world.

On the Dystopian Delta Index my overall score is 6.8, that means I feel that the roots of dystopia have already been established and that we are indeed in the early stage of a dystopian society.

Chapter 29 – Beyond

In my view we have two distinct paths here, but what are they? One is arguably negative; the other is more positive. Apathy is acceptance of the current path towards dystopia I have described in detail earlier in this book, of that I have little doubt.

So, my decision, my chosen path, is to do something about it. My focus is on course correction, and the previous chapters have covered off most of what needs to be said.

We are talking about damage limitation rather than any attempt to create any form of utopia. As I have outlined in this book, the scale of what needs to be fixed is huge.

We need to get to work quickly on changing the mindset of the populace and educating people on the importance of critical thinking. To do that we need to break the current cycle of poor education, lack of deep engagement, and the preference for short-form summarised information and instead encourage the active development of critical thinking skills to help with the identification of lies, mistruths, and manipulation.

We need to stop the rabid division of society and the dehumanisation of people and sectors, and we need to re-engage real human-to-human contact, understanding, and the strengthening of community. This will have to be achieved by using the current social media and news platforms, reclaiming the same tooling that is contributing so heavily to the current decline.

Politicians need to be held to higher standards than they currently are. In the UK we have 'parliamentary privilege', where when an MP or Peer speaks during a proceeding in Parliament they are protected by absolute privilege, meaning they cannot be sued, prosecuted, or held in contempt of court for what they say. According to Carruthers Law, 'absolute privilege in defamation is a complete defence. When a statement is protected by absolute privilege, no defamation claim can succeed in respect of it. This remains true even if the statement is entirely false or was made with malice.' Just think that through; you cannot be held accountable if you lie in Parliament! Our laws need to reflect the modern world; questions need to be raised as to why rules like this still exist. What purpose does it serve when a member of Parliament can say what they like in Parliament with no repercussion. Politicians should be held fully accountable for anything they say or state in public. If advisors provide them with information, then it is their responsibility to make sure that information is sourced and presented correctly. If it is misleading or a lie it needs to be corrected at the point in time. I would love to see an AI service that runs on your TV, tablet, or phone as an independent fact checker. It would identify when incorrect statements are made, display a warning triangle or other symbol to visually indicate it is not correct, and possibly bring up the actual quote or statistics from official source.

Can you imagine the power of that? A politician in the UK claims at a conference that many of the issues faced in the UK are because we are overrun by immigrants arriving on small boats, when suddenly a warning triangle pops up with '*This statement may be misleading – Data source: Gov UK Immigration Asylum Seeker Statistics 2024: small boats: 37,000; legal channels: 71,000*'.

Now that would be a real slap across the face of politicians who want to lie and manipulate. Of course, it's a big ask, but imagine all major social and media platforms being fact checked on the fly. I'm in... and if this ever makes it to *Dragons Den*, remember where you first heard it!

Whether this concept is possible or not, politicians and those with power or influence need to be held accountable, and quickly. If someone makes a racist, sexist, or other -ist comment to incite violence or hate, they must be held accountable at that point in time.

How can we counter the corruption rife within society and in politics? Imagine if, when a politician is making a statement in the House of Commons about the privatisation of healthcare or affordable housing, their financial and commercial interests were displayed on the screen at the same time? '*We should increase the rights of landlords to evict no-fault tenants*', *says MP X who owns 12 rental properties in central London.* Would that sway your opinion? Or maybe MP Y is telling the House of Commons that green energy is a bad choice for the country whilst holding stocks and shares in fossil fuel companies, or that the NHS is failing whilst being a non-exec director of a private healthcare company. I feel that would be a very powerful tool for the world. Assuming that the logistics could be fathomed out.

You could apply that kind of logic across the board calling out racist, sexist, or homophobic language. The possibilities are endless.

The populace needs to see that they are being lied to and manipulated; partly that may be addressed by using technology to fight against technology, but it also needs to be providing people with the right skills.

I recently saw an interview where an Israeli politician was being asked about the killing of children in Gaza. Their answer was that 'they are our enemies'. The reporter asked again, emphasising that these were primary school-aged children and asking how much of a threat they could be; the answer came back once again 'they are our enemies'. The politician had no interest in the rights or wrongs, in their mind additional information about the ages was of no concern. We are seeing this blind adherence here in the UK too. It's the small boats, the LGBTQ+ lot, the lefties, the vegans, women, people named Geoff who own cats, you name it. Belligerence and the lack of desire to seek the truth is almost wholly responsible for the route we are taking.

If we were all to apply critical thinking, challenge information we are presented with, and were more determined to seek the truth, the world would be a very different place.

Picture this example set of scenarios:

Statement – Muslims don't integrate with others

Response – In what context? How many Muslims do you know and speak to regularly? Have you met many and learned about their society and faith?

Statement – Small boats and immigration are the problem

Response – That's a very generic statement; what led you to that conclusion? How many people do you think we are talking about here? Do you know the numbers? Do you know what happens to them when they arrive in the UK?

Statement – Asylum seekers are given hundreds of pounds to live on, mobile phones and Sky TV

Response – That doesn't sound right, let's just check that quickly and see what they are actually entitled to.

I'm sure you can think of many others. We need to think like this far more often than we currently do.

Creating future generations who are cognitively skilled, open minded, and engaged, will, in the long term, resolve many of these issues we face. We must create a populace that cares about the truth, not part of the truth, not one side or one interpretation of it, but the actual truth.

We must fight against discrimination, discriminatory laws and the dehumanisation of people.

For this to work, we have some core human traits to overcome. A key trait is pigeonholing. As humans, we do love a label or a box. How many of our issues come from this desire to label things and people.

White / Black / Asian, Catholic / Church of England / Baptist, Sikh / Muslim / Hindu, Male / Female, Straight / LGBTQ+, Conservative / Labour / Green / LibDem, Left-wing / Right-wing, Football / Rugby / Tennis, Men's sport / Women's sport, Liverpool / Arsenal / Crystal Palace, ADHD / Neurodivergent / Autistic...

What are we doing here? We're creating divisions; we're pigeonholing people and putting them in boxes so we can categorise and label them because that is what we like to do. However, when you create divisions, you also create voids that can be exploited and manipulated at will. What if I wasn't pigeonholed as a male, white British, middle-class, homeowner, husband, father, employed, taxpayer, etc., what if I was just a person. What if that person over there wasn't 'trans', what if they were just 'Alison', who worked and paid taxes like everyone else? The more we label, the more reasons we give to see people as different from us.

As humans we must bring all these things together if we are to resist the drift into a full dystopian world. We must capitalise on the human ability to collaborate and show tolerance. When I have built business teams in the past, it is not with people who agree with me, it is with people who will challenge my thinking, who have different viewpoints and opinions; people who will stand up to me in order to ensure that better, overall decisions are made. It is our ability to work together that has made us so successful as a species, not our ability to fight and argue.

Each of us need to open our eyes to what we are walking into and create our own strategies to develop conscious engagement. We can correct our course, but one person writing a book is not enough, this takes real and rapid action from a wide group of people. It needs a movement.

Chapter 30 – Be the Protagonist

As mentioned earlier in this book, all dystopian novels have a protagonist, someone questioning and challenging the system and organisation that rules their lives. Why? Because otherwise those dystopian novels would all be about how miserable and controlled work, life, and general society is. The protagonist is there to open eyes and give hope.

That feels like where we are now. We need protagonists; we need people to challenge the systems, challenge those who seek to abuse power, and challenge those who choose to take-take-take from both the people and the environment.

One thing the three dystopian novels have in common is that the protagonist does not set out to bring down the authority, instead they are stories of realisation and personal revelation. The protagonists are people who have realised that something isn't right.

This book's primary aim is to open people's eyes to the realisation that the world is broken, more broken than it ever has been, and that if we make the decision not to try and fix it we must be prepared to live with the consequences. Those consequences will be harsh and unpleasant for the vast majority of the people, certainly within the developed parts of the world.

Let's recap and summarise:

The communication skills of the populace, especially the emerging generation, are poor, unless you are privileged enough to go to a well-funded and managed school. That impacts relationships and understanding, both in business and society. It also has a major impact on how you communicate with and get the best out of AI. This is closely related to information literacy and how you articulate and analyse responses. A lack of deep engagement is leading to the loss of comprehension of topics and to the superficial understanding of issues or problems. Our lack of critical thinking is allowing for the wider populace to be manipulated. As AI becomes increasingly embedded in society and the workplace our cognitive skill levels are declining. If this decline is arrested it could go a long way to countering misinformation, lies, and manipulation of the truth, allowing us to see beyond the filter bubbles, bias, and political and social lies that are being presented to us on a daily basis.

We have corporate organisations that wield too much power and influence, and big data companies that are far too close to publicly held data. Data that government authorities and agencies have on us should not be made available for commercial purposes as this could allow for the profiling of the populace and further reach into the realms of elitism and dehumanisation of the masses. In the hands of a more authoritarian government this could lead to the categorisation of minorities as 'undesirables'.

We are becoming more reliant on Gen AI, with huge swathes of the populace stating that they 'chucked it into AI' and blindly accepting the responses and information being provided. Cognitive offloading is OK to a certain extent but allowing offloading to become normal and unchecked is dangerous, not only to our own skills, but to society and business. Repeated and unchecked offloading leads to cognitive laziness and can lead to a superficial wisdom that is easily undermined.

When you combine cognitive decline with our love of short-form, shallow engagement, often AI-generated content, you open the door to the mass manipulation of the populace.

This is the same populace that is hooked on reality TV, banal entertainment, and social media; and who display outwardly content and magical lives whilst living a very different reality. We have, in large part, replaced deep and meaningful relationships and learning with quick fix, superficial appeasement.

A new normal is being established where it is OK to state opinions regarding society, famine, race, religion, gender, or status that would not be acceptable to share in civil society. We have a deep and engrained level of societal apathy that allows for politicians and organisations alike to take advantage of us, and to turn us against each other.

Organisations are facing huge skills shortages in innovation, creativity, information literacy, and critical thinking, all of which need to be elevated to be able to operate in AI-enabled business. These same skills are required in society, and the challenge of fixing that is beyond huge. It feels almost impossible to repair an entire society that doesn't want to think about things that require deep engagement and, more importantly, cognitive effort.

Education, politics, and judicial systems all need to be ripped up and rethought, from the very top to the very bottom. Politics needs to move away from the flip-flop, two-party models that we see so frequently throughout the world. Long-term, radical change needs to be established with general agreement for multiple parties. Our governments need to create frameworks and laws that are fit for the next fifty years, and that can move with agility and strong governance.

Businesses need to rethink how they operate, skill, and innovate. Education needs to rethink how the curriculum looks, what is considered important for today's world, how we teach, test, and measure future generations, and society will need to be fought using the very same tools that are contributing so much to the path we find ourselves on.

We need to take better care of the planet and each other, we need to regain our compassion for people and the environment, and we need to push back on pollutants that are created in the name of ease and cost.

And finally, we need to ensure that new technologies and AI solutions are kept in their place and with the right support to ensure that our mental health remains intact. We always need to remember that these are machines, no matter how lifelike they might appear or how great their conversations become. The closer we come to the machines the more personal the level of data collection will be, and that risks exposing people's vulnerabilities in a way, and on a scale, never seen before.

I put in my dedication at the beginning of this book, 'to my wonderful son, Ben, for whom I hope I am wrong', and I do genuinely hope I am wrong, but I also genuinely fear I am not. Of course, this book won't be 100% accurate, but the general decline into mass unemployment, the ease of manipulation, the rewriting and fabrication of truth, the loss of deep engagement, increase in dehumanisation, and so on, are all happening already.

I would be happy to tackle this topic head on with anyone who disagrees, and I am very happy to be proven wrong, but so far, when I broach this topic with anyone, the response seems to be general agreement. The most push back I have had so far was from a more mature member of society saying that our education system was wonderful and that it was preparing the next generations brilliantly.

Making change on this scale takes more than clicking 'Like' on a social media post from Greta Thunberg or changing your avatar to reflect a particular political view. It takes action. Voter turnout in the UK is poor: at the 2024 General Election only 59.7% of eligible voters bothered to vote, so two in five of the country couldn't or, more likely, couldn't be bothered to vote. In local elections the turnout is even lower, with May 2024 seeing a dismal turnout of less than one third. When people complain about the state of the country there can be little sympathy when turnout is so low. I can't believe that 70%

of the people are happy to let the remaining 30% make decisions for them. If you don't vote, don't complain.

Voting is the first step to action; remove the politicians you dislike or the parties you don't trust. If they go against their election promises, which again is very likely, then remove them at the next opportunity. Send clear messages to the candidates that you expect them to keep their word and deliver on what they promised. If you voted someone in on local issues and they change to vote in line with their national party, hold them accountable for their choice to go with party lines instead of what is important to you. We are too passive; we allow people in positions of power, influence, or wealth to get away with it. We must demand greater integrity and authenticity from these people or, as is happening now, the general populace will be trodden on politically, financially, and in all aspects of life.

All of this starts with asking questions. Why? Who benefits? Does that seem right? Where did that information come from? And by demanding change from the people who are there to represent you; they and all authorities and organisations need to be held to account. We need to remember that we are, first and foremost, human, and so is everyone you will meet. For now, anyway. Our bonds as humans are what have allowed us to become so successful as a species.

Every label we apply to a person or group destroys collaborative and cohesive relationships. Humans will be much better off if we align ourselves to fight back against the machines, the people who control them, and those who seek to manipulate us for their own personal gain.

To prevent further decline into A World We Don't Want, we need to change our thinking, hold those with power and influence to account, break down barriers, and create a future based around tolerance, collaboration, truth, and learning.

Unexpected

I wrote this poem in August 2017. I can't recall what the trigger was, but revisiting it after unexpectedly writing this book, it feels like an appropriate way to sign off. It was a personal venture and was never for public consumption; make of it what you will, but it feels like it might be time to share it.

Hope

I am weary.

My heart is tired and dulled.

The childlike hope and wonder of the world, ground down by constant streams of hurt and hate.

That darken our windows and hide the light of this happy accident.

I am weary of being told what I should think and what my opinion should be.

We are taught to look for the bad and the dark, taught to see fault in all and others.

We are fed bad news and shown the pitiful state of the world.

Slowly we are moulded and conditioned to no longer see the great and good.

A World We Don't Want

I am weary until I look into the eyes of the future.

He is unaware and filled with light and love and harbours no prejudice.

The dull and tired are replaced with pride and hope.

We must remember to see and seek the good. We are one people.

Yes, I am weary.

But the future lies with those not yet turned.

We must protect what is right and fair, what is unspoiled and beautiful.

For our children, our world.

I love my child. I shall keep his hope.

Acknowledgements

Writing a book was never on my to do list. It wasn't even on my 'maybe one day' list, and I know that for sure as that list doesn't even exist.

It has been an incredible process, and I have learned so much; but as with so many things, I could not have completed it without help and for that I need to thank a few people.

First, my wife, who has been incredibly tolerant during this process. Having research and observations thrown at her, almost daily, as I discover new facts or studies that have gone to reinforce or challenge my thoughts. She has become a patient yet unwitting hero for a process she never signed up to.

Second is my brother, Richard. He saw there was more to my initial observations, has played the role of devil's advocate in challenging my thoughts, questioning the wisdom of writing a book like this and all whilst being one of my most ardent supporters.

I also wish to thank Rick. He and I first bonded at a presentation where we both identified at least 6 different **fonts** on use in a single slide. He has been my friend, my beta reader and has done himself proud. I can't thank him enough for all the time and effort he has invested in this book.

Kelly from Kemend, my proofreader, formatter and guide throughout this adventure. At times it has been overwhelming, but having a steady hand to lead the way has proven invaluable.

I want to thank my son, Ben. He's done nothing more than be himself, but without my love and concern for him and his future I do wonder whether I would have taken this step forward.

Lastly, I want to thank you for taking the time to read this book. I hope that at the very least, regardless of your personal opinions, it helps raise awareness of one or many of the issues presented along the way.

Together we can change the future. Be the protagonist in your own story.

Works Cited

2025. *Parliament UK.* [Online] May 2025. https://committees.parliament.uk/writtenevidence/141354/pdf/.

Bartley, Kevin. 2025. Rivery. *Rivery.* [Online] 2 May 2025. https://rivery.io/blog/big-data-statistics-how-much-data-is-there-in-the-world.

Bates, Laura. 2025. *The New Age of Sexism.* s.l. : Simon & Schuster, 2025.

Benanav, Aaron. 2020. *Automation and the Future of Work.* s.l. : Verso, 2020.

2022. Cognitive Load Theory. *Medical College of Wisconsin.* [Online] May 2022. https://www.mcw.edu/-/media/MCW/Education/Academic-Affairs/OEI/Faculty-Quick-Guides/Cognitive-Load-Theory.pdf.

Coplin, Dav. 2014. *The Rise of the Humans.* s.l. : Harriman House, 2014.

Dictionary, Cambridge. Cambridge Dictionary. *dictionary.cambridge.org.* [Online] https://dictionary.cambridge.org/dictionary/english/society.

Dobeli, Rolf. 2014. *The Art of Thinking Clearly.* s.l. : Hodder & Stoughton, 2014.

Feffer, John. 2024. FPIF. *FPIF.* [Online] 4 September 2024. https://fpif.org/why-ukraine-invaded-russia/.

Forum, World Economic. 2025. World Economic Forum. *World Economic Forum.* [Online] Jan 2025. https://www.weforum.org/publications/the-future-of-jobs-report-2025.

Gartner. 2025. Employee Anxiety. *Gartner.* [Online] 2025. https://gtnr.it/3Ik2om6.

2023. Goldman Sachs. *www.goldmansachs.com.* [Online] April 2023. https://www.goldmansachs.com/insights/articles/generative-ai-could-raise-global-gdp-by-7-percent.html.

Government, UK. 2025. PM speech on AI Opportunities Action Plan. *www.gov.uk.* [Online] 13 January 2025. https://www.gov.uk/government/speeches/pm-speech-on-ai-opportunities-action-plan-13-january-2025.

Heidt, Jonathan. 2024. *The Anxious Generation.* s.l. : Penguin, 2024.

International, Conservation. 2014. [Online] 2014. https://www.youtube.com/watch?v=WmVLcj-XKnM.

Kwik, Jim. 2023. LinkedIn - Jim Kwik. *LinkedIn.* [Online] 2023. https://www.linkedin.com/posts/jimkwik_if-rip-van-winkle-woke-up-today-after-a-hundred-activity-6974713536723755008-T2g8.

Lucas, George and Edwards, Gareth. 2016. *Rogue One: A Star Wars Story.* 2016.

Morson. 2020. Morson. *Morson.com.* [Online] 10 October 2020. https://www.morson.com/cbi-warns-uk-90-percent-of-uk-workforce-will-need-new-skills-by-2030.

Nations, United. 2025. United Nations. *www.un.org.* [Online] 2025. https://www.un.org/en/global-issues/population.

Ofcom. 2024. News Consumption in the UK 2924. *Ofcom.* [Online] 10 September 2024. https://www.ofcom.org.uk/siteassets/resources/documents/research-and-data/tv-radio-and-on-demand-research/tv-research/news/news-consumption-2024/news-consumption-in-the-uk-2024-report.pdf.

Office, Home. 2024. GOV UK Immigration Statistics . [Online] 2024. https://www.gov.uk/government/statistics/immigration-system-statistics-year-ending-december-2024/summary-of-latest-statistics.

Pirsig, Robert M. 1974. *Zen and the Art of Motorcycle Maintenance* . s.l. : Transworld Publishers Ltd, 1974.

Talmage-Rostron, Mark. 2025. Nexford University. *www.nexford.edu.* [Online] June 2025. https://www.nexford.edu/insights/how-will-ai-affect-jobs.

Wikipedia. Wikipedia. *OSI Model.* [Online] https://en.wikipedia.org/wiki/OSI_model.

About the Author

I'm certainly not normal, that has been confirmed by many people over the years, but I am nothing special. I hold no high-ranking academic qualifications, and I have not spent thirty years researching this as a topic. I am a technical consultant of over twenty-five years, married to a lovely woman, father to a fabulous child, have two dogs and live in the countryside. I was, however, fortunate enough to have a great education, not that my exams reflected that, but that's a different story. I've worked in both the public and private sectors, for small and large organisations, and for good and bad employers. I've travelled a reasonable amount for both work and pleasure, lived in France for a while, and I have encountered wonderful, interesting people, and a not insubstantial number of wholly, wilfully ignorant, and thoroughly unpleasant people.

Today, I help businesses navigate the changing technical world, not so much the shiny solutions, but how their organisations, leadership and workforces need to adapt to thrive in a world with advancing technologies, including AI. I am very aware of the world around me, and I take time to consider and understand how these advancements impact society.

Since starting this adventure, my brain has hardly stopped trying to work things out; it has been a real rollercoaster of emotions, despondency and hope. The main driver for me was that, ultimately, this is not the vision of a world I want my son to live in. It is likely too late to fix it for my generation's benefit, but for future generations it is something I believe we have to try and resolve, and the first step is making people aware of the challenge.

As mentioned, I am not anything special and I think that statement is of considerable importance. I have made huge mistakes, got things horribly wrong, said things that make me ashamed, hurt people, and been a general knob at times. I have bumbled my way through much of my life, like most people, but I like to think that I have corrected all of those things with the realisation of my mistakes. So, no, I am not special. I am not a professor of this or that, I am not academic, I am not an established author or some internationally renowned business mogul. I am a typical human being, not perfect, but an average, run of the mill human, and that is incredibly important because it is everyday people like me who are required to help change the course of the future.

I believe that as humans it is us who will need to alter the way we live to avoid falling into the trap of a full dystopian world. My writing of this book feels like it is a deep-rooted concern that has suddenly been elevated to the forefront of my purpose. It is time to wake people up and open their eyes to what is going on.

www.ingramcontent.com/pod-product-compliance
Lightning Source LLC
LaVergne TN
LVHW100257210926
848480LV00003B/949
* 9 7 8 1 9 1 9 3 7 9 2 0 3 *